JOSHUA

The LORD, The People, The Land, The Law

A Bible Study

C. V. Kirkstadt

LARGE PRINT VERSION

ISBN 970-0-9982088-0-0 (Paperback)
ISBN 978-0-9982088-4-8 (Paperback – LARGE Print version)
Kindle Version ASIN: B0821RLJQM

Published by CVKPress, Loveland, Colorado

Contents

Truehearted, Wholehearted
Trust and Obey
God of our Fathers
I Love to Tell the Story

Commentaries
Books, Articles and DVDs

Acknowledgements

Thank you to the Martha Circle at Mountain View Presbyterian Church. In 2009, we used the Horizons Study Guide to learn about The Book of Joshua. I was the study leader.

Thank you to my parents who raised me on Christian principles. They were excellent role models. By following their advice I am sure I have avoided many problems plus I can meet adversity and the challenges in life.

Thank you to Paula Dumont, Kathryn Churchill, Carol Terrell, Donna Fullerton, and Jim Webb who helped me edit this study guide.

Thanks to Holy Spirit, your help and encouragement are a constant blessing.

This large print version of "*JOSHUA: The LORD, The People, The Land, The Law*" was originally published February 2017.

Minor changes to this large print version have been made so it is consistent with the Paperback version ISBN 970-0-9982088-0-0.

February 2019

Introduction

Welcome to this study of the Book of Joshua, found in the Old Testament.

The Book of Joshua describes major events in the formation of the nation of Israel. The 12 tribes of Israel under the leadership of Moses and directed by God have been in the desert for 40 years. At the end of Deuteronomy, the Israelites are in Moab just east of the Jordan River. Moses bids farewell and designates Joshua the new leader as God has directed (Deuteronomy 31:1-6).

Old Testament study regarding the Book of Joshua has evolved. In the early 1900's the conclusions were that the book was written hundreds of years after the events based on oral tradition. Also some archeologists have concluded that events like the battle of Jericho never happened. More recent archeology findings have concluded that, yes, the events did occur.

The Book of Joshua is well worth your time to study. This study will focus on highlights in the Book of Joshua. For further study, several commentaries that give a verse by verse analysis are listed in the Bibliography.

This guide can be used for individual study or with a group. It is suggested you read the Scripture References and the Additional Information in this study before you try to answer the Questions.

This Bible Study is designed for everybody.

For Christians, the Questions and Additional Information will challenge you to look deeper into your beliefs. God has amazing things in store for you.

For those who are not Christians, the Book of Joshua can be an opportunity to learn about God. Also be sure to study the "Good News" information (see Contents).

For everybody....are you ready to "Cross the Jordan"?

Suggestions for Individual Study

1. Preparation - besides this study guide, you will need a Bible. The scripture quoted in the study is from the New King James Version. It is also suggested, if your Bible is not a Study Bible, to use a Bible Atlas and a commentary on the Book of Joshua.

2. Read the entire Book of Joshua.

3. For each lesson:

   A. Start with prayer, listen for what God may be telling you.

   B. Read the Scripture

   C. Read the Questions to get familiar with them, then read the Additional Information.

   D. After reading the Scripture, the Questions and the Additional Information, answer the Questions using the space provided to write your answers.

   E. End with prayer or sing the suggested hymn.

Suggestions for Group Study
(for the Group Leader)

Suggested Preparation for each Lesson

Read the Scripture, the Questions and the Additional Information.

Try to answer the Questions.

Suggested Agenda for each Lesson:

Open with prayer

Allow 25-30 minutes for the questions you have selected to discuss. Be selective. Select 2-3 questions you plan to use for discussion.

Allow 5-10 minutes for additional discussion

Summarize.

Close with a prayer and/or sing the suggested hymn.

Suggestions to Facilitate Learning

For this first meeting, ask the people in the group to introduce themselves.

Begin each lesson with a short introduction and read the scripture.

Stay on one topic. If someone brings up a new topic, make a note of it and say you would like to save this for later. Include time at the end of your study time to cover these items.

Room Setup

If possible have people sit in a circle so everyone can see and communicate with each other

General Guidelines for Questions

Start with an easy question regarding the facts (What? When? Where? Who?)

When asking a question, wait a good 60 seconds for a response, if no response then re-phrase the question.

If you get a long answer, you may want to summarize, for example, "so what you are saying is..."

Lesson 1: Background - Historical and Literary Context

SCRIPTURE:

Genesis 15:1-21
Genesis 17:1-27
Deuteronomy 34:1-12
Joshua 1:1-9

OBJECTIVES:

Review the history of the time and the people involved.

The Book of Joshua tells of a major event in the history of the Israelites. An overview of relevant history is useful.

QUESTIONS:

1. List key events in the history of the Israelites.

2. What is the meaning of a "Covenant"? What was God's Covenant with the Israelites? What is the history of God's promise about The Land?

3. Who wrote the book of Joshua?
   Would the Israelites have written records from this period?
   What writing system would have been used?

4. List the people and places of significance at the time the Israelites arrived. Who were they?

ADDITIONAL INFORMATION:

History of the Israelites (Old Testament)

A long time ago (about 2000 BCE) a man named Abram received a call from the LORD, *"Leave your country, your people and your father's household and go to the land I will show you."* Abram took his wife and all his possessions and set out for the land of Canaan. At Shechem he built an altar to the LORD. (Genesis 12:1-7)

The LORD gives Abram a new name, Abraham. (Genesis 17:5) Abraham and Sara have a son named Isaac. (Genesis 21:1-7) Both Abraham and his wife, Sara are buried at Hebron. Isaac marries Rebekah and they have twins: Jacob and Esau. (Genesis 25:21-26) Jacob has twelve sons. (Genesis 35:23-26)

Joseph, one of Jacob's sons is sold into slavery in Egypt by his brothers. (Genesis 37:12-36) Some time later Jacob (also known as Israel) and his family move to Egypt due to famine in Canaan.

Circumstances changed for the Israelites and they become slaves to the Egyptians. (Exodus 1:1-22) The LORD sends a man named Moses to lead the Israelites out of bondage. (Exodus 3:1-22)

The Passover followed by the Exodus (about 1450 BCE) of the Israelites from Egypt is a major event for the Israelites. (Exodus 12:1–14:31)

Leaving Egypt, the Israelites cross the Red Sea. At Mt. Sinai Moses receives the 10 commandments. (Exodus 19:1–20:17)

About a year later they arrive at Kadesh and spies are sent out to scout the Promised Land. When the spies return only Joshua and Caleb have an encouraging report. (Numbers 13:1-33) The rest said it was a good land but the people living there were too strong.

So the Israelites remained in the wilderness. (Numbers 14:1-35) They took 40 years to arrive on the eastern shore of the Jordan River.

Joshua leads the Israelites into Canaan (about 1406 BCE).

The LORD was with Joshua and his men. They were successful in defeating many people in Canaan.

The Covenant is renewed at Shechem. (Joshua 24:25-26)

The Book of Judges tells about events after Joshua's time (a period of about 400 years). The Israelites were unable to drive out all of the Canaanites. The Israelites were influenced by the pagan practices of the Canaanites. When difficulties arose the LORD raised up judges.

The Israelites ask for a king. Samuel warns the people, telling them the words of the LORD regarding what the king who will reign over them will do. (1 Samuel 8:1-22)

In 1000 BC, David is anointed king over Israel at Hebron. David and his men capture Jerusalem. (2 Samuel 5:6-7)

Solomon, David's son builds the first temple in Jerusalem, 480 years after the Israelites came out of Egypt. (1 Kings 6:1)

After Solomon, the kingdom is divided: Israel, the northern kingdom and Judah, the southern kingdom.

In 722 BCE, Israel falls to Assyria. (2 Kings 17:1-41) The Northern Tribes are deported to Assyria.

In 586 BCE (about 400 years after David's reign), Judah falls to Babylonia. The temple and Jerusalem are destroyed and the inhabitants of Judah are deported to Babylon. (2 Kings 25:1-21)

In 538 BCE Cyrus of Persia conquers Babylonia. The Jews, who have been in exile in Babylon for 70 years, are allowed to return to Jerusalem and rebuild the temple. (Ezra 1:1-11)

What is a covenant?

A covenant is an agreement between two parties. In the Near Eastern culture, a covenant described a relationship. Both parties were expected to fulfill their commitments, with penalties described if the agreement was not observed.

God's promise about The Land

God's covenants with Abram/Abraham.

> *And it came to pass, when the sun went down and it was dark, that behold, there appeared a smoking oven and a burning torch that passed between those pieces. On the same day the LORD made a covenant with Abram, saying: "To your descendants I have given this land, from the river of Egypt to the great river, the River Euphrates." (Genesis 15:18)*

> *"And I will establish My covenant between Me and you and your descendants after you in their generations, for an everlasting covenant, to be God to you and your descendants after you. Also I give to you and your descendants after you the land in which you are a stranger, **all the land of Canaan, as an everlasting possession**; and I will be their God." And God said to Abraham: "As for you, you shall keep My covenant, you and your descendants after you throughout their generations. This is My covenant which you shall keep, between Me and you and your descendants after you: Every male child among you shall be circumcised; and you shall be circumcised in the flesh of your foreskins, and it shall be a sign of the covenant between Me and you." (Genesis 17:7-11)*

Abraham is promised a son.

> *"Then God said: "No, Sarah your wife shall bear you a son, and you shall call his name Isaac; I will establish My covenant with him for an everlasting covenant, and with his descendants after him." (Genesis 17:19)*

Many years after this agreement, God renews the covenant with the descendants of Abraham at Mt Sinai. God describes his rules and requirements. Both blessings and curses are associated with this agreement.

> *"After the death of Moses the servant of the LORD, it came to pass that the LORD spoke to Joshua the son of Nun, Moses' assistant, saying: "Moses My servant is dead. Now therefore, arise, go over this Jordan, you and all this people, to the land which I am giving to them--the children of Israel. Every place that the sole of your foot will tread upon I have given you, as I said to Moses. **From the wilderness and this Lebanon as far as the great river, the River Euphrates, all the land of the Hittites, and to the Great Sea toward the going down of the sun, shall be your territory.** No man shall be able to stand before you all the days of your*

life; as I was with Moses, so I will be with you. I will not leave you nor forsake you. Be strong and of good courage, for to this people you shall divide as an inheritance the land which I swore to their fathers to give them. Only be strong and very courageous, that you may observe to do according to all the law which Moses My servant commanded you; do not turn from it to the right hand or to the left, that you may prosper wherever you go." (Joshua 1:1-7)

Who wrote Joshua?

Tradition says the book was written by Joshua. Chapter 24 was added after his death.

Here are comments by John Bright.

> "the editor did not invent his material, but merely worked over material of great antiquity and value."
> History is "written to illustrate the dealing of God with his people"
> "in history is God revealed, in history are his gracious acts and judgments made manifest." [1]

The version of the Book of Joshua we have today went through various revisions. The initial version was probably written sometime after Joshua's death, but before the monarchy. Then it underwent a revision during the reign of King Josiah (640 - 609 BCE). Some additional material may have been added later. [2]

Writing Systems

About 200 years ago, various people started to question the validity of the stories in the Bible. The content of the first five books of the Bible (Genesis, Exodus, Leviticus, Numbers, and Deuteronomy) was characterized as legend and/or folklore. The assumption was that the text of the Bible was not written down until the 8th century BCE.

However, in recent archeology discoveries, many examples of written records date to the time of the Exodus and in fact go back to at least 2300 BCE. Since Moses was trained in the Egyptian court as a young man, it is not difficult to believe that Moses was prepared by God to compile the history as described in Genesis and to write the laws and requirements given to him by God. These documents were then brought by the Israelites into Canaan at the time of Joshua.

Moses also lived with his father-in-law, Jethro (a priest of Midian), another source of information.

> So the sacred book of the Christian and Jewish faiths had its origin, not in folk-lore and legends of ancient times collected and edited by some priestly dignitary in the 8th B.C. century, but in the painstaking work of men of God who lived in the dawn of history, setting down their stories in archaic forms of writing which had to be translated and copied time and again in new and different characters, even before Abraham saw them. It has been

abundantly demonstrated in this our day that the stories of the Old Testament are factually true, the work of men who knew the facts and lived within measurable time of the events they recorded.[3]

People living in the Land

In addition to people living in Canaan, there were major civilizations at the time of the conquest: Egyptians, Babylonians, Hittites, and Assyrians.

There were Canaanites, Hittites, Hivites, Perizzites, Girgashites, Amorites, Jebusites living in the Land. (Joshua 3:10)

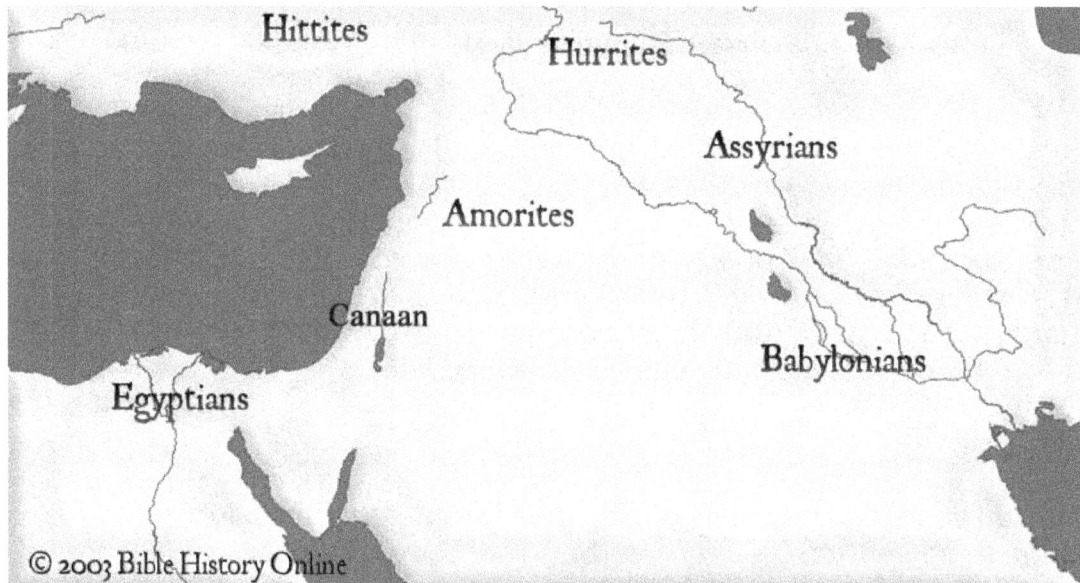

© 2003 Bible History Online

NOTES:

1. Bright, John. "The Book of Joshua – Introduction and Exegesis". *The Interpreter's Bible, Volume 2,* (Abingdon Press, 1953), 546, 548

2. Wright, G. Ernest. "JOSHUA - a New Translation with Introduction and Commentary". *Anchor Bible – Volume 6,* edited by William Foxwell Albright and David Noel Freedman, (Doubleday, 1982). 132-133

3. *The Antiquity of the Books of Moses (Booklet 07).* Herald of Christ's Kingdom (the official publication of the Pastoral Bible Institute) https://herald-magazine.com/bookstore-2/the-antiquity-of-the-books-of-moses/. Accessed 18 November 2016.

Lesson 2: What do we know about Joshua?

SCRIPTURE:

Joshua 1:5-9
Joshua 1:16-18

OBJECTIVE:

Learn about God's version of leadership

One of the main characteristics of Joshua was his belief that he must "ask for the LORD's direction" before taking action.

SUGGESTED HYMN:

Truehearted, Wholehearted

QUESTIONS:

1. What do you know about Joshua? What had Joshua seen and experienced that would help him believe and trust in the LORD?

2. What is meant by God directed leadership?

3. What qualities do we look for in our leaders today?
   in our church
   in our community
   in our government

4. Do you believe God appoints leaders for a specific task?
   Give examples.

5. Describe the interaction between the LORD and Joshua, Joshua and the Israelites.

ADDITIONAL INFORMATION:

About Joshua:

Joshua was a young man when he left Egypt and spent 40 years in the wilderness. He was probably about 60 years old when he was chosen by the LORD to lead the Israelites into Canaan. After a lifetime of faithful service Joshua died at age 110. (Joshua 24:29) Joshua had many experiences to help him believe and trust the LORD.

Joshua was a slave in Egypt.

Joshua experienced the Passover and witnessed crossing the Red Sea. (Numbers 32:11-12)

Joshua fought the Amalekites as Moses had ordered.

> *Now Amalek came and fought with Israel in Rephidim. And Moses said to Joshua, "Choose us some men and go out, fight with Amalek. Tomorrow I will stand on the top of the hill with the rod of God in my hand." So Joshua did as Moses said to him, and fought with Amalek. (Exodus 17:8-10)*

Joshua was aid to Moses. He was with Moses on the mountain of God.

> *So Moses arose with his assistant Joshua, and Moses went up to the mountain of God. (Exodus 24:13)*

Joshua guarded the tent of meeting. (Exodus 33:11)

Joshua was one of spies chosen to explore Canaan. Joshua and Caleb bring back a favorable report. (Numbers 13 and 14)

The LORD orders Joshua to be commissioned. (Numbers 27:18-21)

Joshua is chosen by God to lead the Israelites into Canaan. (Deuteronomy 1:38, 3:28)

The people agree to obey Joshua. (Joshua 1:16-17)

Joshua instructs the people to serve the LORD. (Joshua 24:1-27)

Joshua tells all the Israelites where he stands.

> *"But as for me and my house, we will serve the LORD." (Joshua 24:15b)*

About Leadership

Here are some questions about evaluating our leaders.

What do we know about their background?

Who were their mentors (for example, Joshua worked with Moses for many years)?

What qualities, what experiences shape their views?

Where do they turn to for advice and counsel?

What do you know about what leaders have actually accomplished?

> *"For a good tree does not bear bad fruit, nor does a bad tree bear good fruit. For every tree is known by its own fruit. For men do not gather figs from thorns, nor do they gather grapes from a bramble bush. A good man out of the good treasure of his heart brings forth good; and an evil man out of the evil treasure of his heart brings forth evil. For out of the abundance of the heart his mouth speaks."* (Luke 6:43-45)

Communication

Study Joshua to learn about effective communication. First he communicates with God, once he has his "marching orders" he communicates the plans to his people.

The LORD encourages Joshua with three promises:

1. You will cross the Jordan, you and all the people.
2. I will be with you.
3. You will apportion the land to each tribe as its inheritance.

Transparency and consistency are hallmarks of good leadership. Joshua repeatedly reminds the people what the LORD has done and is doing for them.

Lesson 3: Crossing the Jordan

SCRIPTURE:

Joshua 3:1–5:12

OBJECTIVE:

Learn about preparation and remembering what God has done for us.

Understand the meaning of "Crossing the Jordan"

QUESTIONS:

1. The Israelites prepare to enter The Land, what actually happened?

2. Why were the Israelites circumcised?

3. Especially at major turning points in our lives, do we take time to remember and make proper preparations for the road ahead?

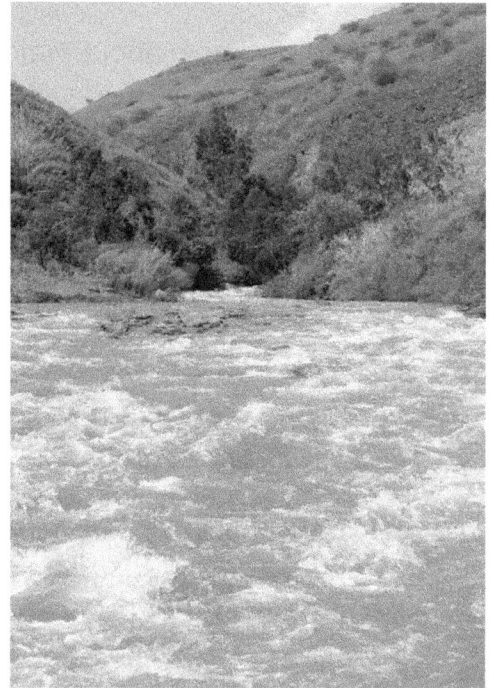

4. What events do we celebrate that help us remember what God has done for us?
Example: Passover, Lord's Supper

5. Is "Crossing the Jordan" an example of a great spiritual truth? Have you had a "Crossing the Jordan" experience?

ADDITIONAL INFORMATION:

How many crossed the Jordan?

The census taken prior to crossing into Canaan counted about 600,000 men 20 years or older who are able to serve in the army of Israel.

> *So Moses and Eleazar the priest spoke with them in the plains of Moab by the Jordan, across from Jericho, saying: "Take a census of the people from twenty years old and above, just as the LORD commanded Moses and the children of Israel who came out of the land of Egypt."* (Numbers 26:3-4)

Including women and children about 1 million Israelites crossed the Jordan. Only the fighting men from the tribes of Ruben, Gad and Manasseh crossed over. (Joshua 4:12-13)

Highlights before and after crossing the Jordan River

Preparation events. (Joshua 3:1 -5:12)

The priests leading with the ark "set foot in Jordan", the water flow stops.

The Israelites cross on dry ground.

Twelve stones are set up as a memorial at Gilgal.

The men are circumcised.

They celebrate Passover.

The people of Jericho are fearful (action by God as part of preparation).

> "The Israelites remained at the edge of the Jordan for three days. This, no doubt, was necessary to enable them to make provisions for such a large contingent of people and families to cross the swollen stream. But the delay also taught Israel to wait for God's direction. How could this large company of people cross the Jordan without God's help? **In the springtime the normally narrow river flooded its banks so that it filled its depression valley that was 150 feet deep and as much as a mile wide.**" [1]

About Circumcision

Circumcision was a sign of the covenant between God and Abraham and his descendants. (Genesis 17:11)

About Importance of Remembering

Crossing the Jordan is a major milestone for God's people. The priests, carrying the Ark of the Covenant, lead the people. God stops the flow of water. Joshua commands that 12 stones be setup as a memorial.

> *"Then he spoke to the children of Israel, saying: "When your children ask their fathers in time to come, saying, 'What are these stones?' then you shall let your children know, saying, 'Israel crossed over this Jordan on dry land'; for the LORD your God dried up the waters of the Jordan before you until you had crossed over, as the LORD your God did to the Red Sea, which He dried up before us until we had crossed over, that all the peoples of the earth may know the hand of the LORD, that it is mighty, that you may fear the LORD your God forever." (Joshua 4:21-24)*

In today's world, these words from Deuteronomy are still relevant. If we do not pass the stories and lessons down to the next generation, the stories are lost. The role of repetition and ritual in passing on "the story" is essential.

> *"Hear, O Israel: The LORD our God, the LORD is one!*
> *You shall love the LORD your God with all your heart,*
> *with all your soul, and with all your strength.*
> *"And these words which I command you today shall be in your heart.*
> *You shall teach them diligently to your children,*
> *and shall talk of them when you sit in your house,*
> *when you walk by the way, when you lie down, and when you*
> *rise up.*
> *You shall bind them as a sign on your hand,*
> *and they shall be as frontlets between your eyes.*
> *You shall write them on the doorposts of your house and on your gates*
> (Deuteronomy 6:4-9)

Guidelines for teaching the People

In addition to documenting the law, God made provision for all the people to be instructed.

> *So Moses wrote this law and delivered it to the priests, the sons of Levi, who bore the ark of the covenant of the LORD, and to all the elders of Israel. And Moses commanded them, saying: "At the end of every seven years, at the appointed time in the year of release, at the Feast of Tabernacles, when all Israel comes to appear before the LORD your God in the place which He chooses, you shall read this law before all Israel in their hearing.*
>
> *Gather the people together, men and women and little ones, and the stranger who is within your gates, that they may hear and that they may learn to fear the LORD your God and carefully observe all the words of this law, and that their children, who have not known it, may hear and learn to fear the LORD your God as long as you live in the land which you cross the Jordan to possess." (Deuteronomy 31:9-13)*

Benefits of Total Commitment – New Testament Perspective

In his study guide, Warren W. Wiersbe reminds us that

> The Book of Joshua tells us how to be victorious soldiers and how to claim our rich spiritual inheritance in Jesus Christ. It tells us how to be strong and courageous as we face our enemies and march forward to claim new territory for the LORD."[2]

In his study guide, Wiersbe describes four geographic locations seen in the history of Israel that illustrate four spiritual experiences[3]:

Egypt (Egypt was the place of death and bondage from which Israel was delivered),

The Wilderness (Israelites lived in unbelief and disobedience),

Canaan (model for the Christian life - conflict and victory, faith and obedience, spiritual riches and rest), and

Babylon (Israel in captivity due to disobedience and worshiping the idols of the pagan nations around them).

Where are you living?

About Crossing the Jordan

A special land has been promised by God for the Israelites but in order to claim their inheritance they must act.

After the Israelites experience the events of the Exodus and receive the law at Mt. Sinai they arrive at Kadish in the Desert of Paran. A team is sent out to explore the land of Canaan. Only Joshua and Caleb return with a recommendation to *"go up at once and take possession of the land"* (Numbers 13:30). In spite of all these people had witnessed of God's provision for them they did not have the faith to act, as a result the Israelites continued to stay in the wilderness for 40 years. (Numbers 14:30-35)

At the Jordan, the people obey God's instructions and "cross the Jordan." (Joshua 3:1-17) As a result they successfully occupy the land.

Some Christian songs have equated Israel's crossing the Jordan with the believer's dying and going to heaven, example – "Swing Low, Sweet Chariot". "The events recorded in the Book of Joshua have to do with the life of God's people and not their death! The Book of Joshua records battles, defeats, sins, and failures - none of which will take place in heaven, This book illustrates how believers today can say good-bye to the old life and enter into their rich inheritance in Jesus Christ."[4]

We need to be aware that God has plans for us, but we need to step out and trust He will be with us as we proceed.

NOTES:

1. Enns, Paul P., *Joshua: Bible Study Commentary*, (Grand Rapids, MI: Zondervan, 1981) 36

2. Wiersbe, Warren W., *Be Strong – Putting God's Power to Work in Your Life,* (Colorado Springs: David C. Cook, 1993), Preface

3. Wiersbe, 17-19.

4. Wiersbe, 16-17.

Lesson 4: The Battle at Jericho

SCRIPTURE:

Joshua 5:13 - 6:27

OBJECTIVE:

What happened? Did it happen?

SUGGESTED HYMN:

Trust and Obey

QUESTIONS:

1. How do you think the people of Israel felt when Joshua gave them the strange battle plan? How would walking around the city and blowing the shofars accomplish their objective? How do you think you would have responded?

2. Have you ever heard the sound of a shofar?

3. What was significant of the Ark and Priests leading the assembly around Jericho? What were the factors that led to success?

4. Was there really a battle at Jericho? Describe the archeological evidence for the destruction of Jericho.

ADDITIONAL INFORMATION:

The Battle Plan

Now Jericho was securely shut up because of the children of Israel; none went out, and none came in. And the LORD said to Joshua: "See! I have given Jericho into your hand, its king, and the mighty men of valor. You shall march around the city, all you men of war; you shall go all around the city once. This you shall do six days. And seven priests shall bear seven trumpets of rams' horns before the ark. But the seventh day you shall march around the city seven times, and the priests shall blow the trumpets. It shall come to pass, when they make a long blast with the ram's horn, and when you hear the sound of the trumpet, that all the people shall shout with a great shout; then the wall of the city will fall down flat. And the people shall go up every man straight before him." (Joshua 6:1-5)

About trumpets (Shofars)

The trumpets used by the priests were curved ram's horns called shofars; these horns produced loud, far-reaching tones. The shofar was important in the religious life of Israel as it was sounded each Friday evening to announce the beginning of the Sabbath. It was also sounded in proclaiming the Feast of Trumpets (Lev 23:24) that has great prophetic significance (Isaiah 27:13; Joel 2:1). The sound of the trumpets in Joshua 6 was the announcement of blessing in the land which the LORD their God was giving them. [1]

To hear the sound of a Shofar watch this video – *Shofar Blowing – Elohim's Trumpets* [2]

Some information about the Ark of the Covenant

The Ark signified the presence of the LORD. It also signified His covenant, which means His commitment to His promises as well as the obligations of Israel. The Ark contained the two tablets of the Testimony (The Ten Commandments).

God tells Moses to make an Ark (box) to hold "the Testimony" - the Ten Commandments. (Exodus 25:10-22, 40:20)

God also orders a "Tabernacle" (tent) to house the Ark. Both the Ark and the Tabernacle were portable and went with the people. The Ark and the Tabernacle were symbols of God's presence with the people.

The Priests carrying the Ark led the Israelites as they crossed the Jordan to enter the land of Canaan. (Joshua 3:14)

The Ark was again carried by the Priests at the battle of Jericho. (Joshua 6:6-8)

After the conquest, the Ark and the Tabernacle were set up in Shiloh. (Joshua 18:1)

Later the Ark was captured by the Philistines. The Philistines were struck with a plague. They decided to send the Ark back to the Israelites. (1 Samuel 5:1-7:1)

King David moved the Ark to Jerusalem. After the First Temple was built by David's son, Solomon, the Ark was placed in the Temple. (2 Chronicles 5:7-10)

The last mention of the Ark in the Bible is during the reign of King Josiah.

> "Then he (Josiah) said to the Levites who taught all Israel, who were holy to the LORD; "Put the Holy Ark in the house which Solomon the son of David, king of Israel, built." (2 Chronicles 35:3)

Since there is no mention about the Ark being carried off to Babylon at the fall of Jerusalem, there is speculation that the Ark was hidden somewhere in Jerusalem.

Another explanation, can be found in the Book of 2 Maccabees 2:4-5[3]

> "It was also in the writing that the prophet, having received an oracle, ordered that the tent and the ark should follow with him, and that he went out to the mountain where Moses had gone up and had seen the inheritance of God. And Jeremiah came and found a cave, and he brought there the tent and the ark and the altar of incense, and he sealed up the entrance.

Role of the Ark and the Priests

The Ark was a symbol of the presence of God. The Priests were the caretakers of this important artifact. What is the symbolic significance of the Ark and the Priests leading the warriors into battle?

Regarding the Battle at Jericho and the Conquest: did it really happen?

For many years the problems of correlating chronology of historical events with the biblical chronology of early Israelite history led to questions about the historical accuracy of the events recorded in the Bible. Much of the difficulty is based on assumptions about Egyptian and Hittite chronology and events in Canaan.

In the late 1980's David Rohl put forward several unconventional theories revising the chronology of Ancient Egypt and Israel to form an alternative new chronology. The proposed new chronology placed the Exodus around 1450 BC, and Solomon's reign in the Late Bronze Age (not the Iron Age).[4]

For instance the conventional chronology assumes that Ramesses II was Pharaoh at the time of the Exodus. Rohl gives compelling evidence that the Pharaoh was Dudimose at the time of the Exodus.[5] Rohl says that Ramesses II who is referred to as Shishak in the Bible (1 Kings 14:25-26), was a contemporary of Solomon.[6]

Rohl's analysis is consistent with information found in the Bible.

> *And it came to pass in the four hundred and eightieth year after the children of Israel had come out of the land of Egypt, in the fourth year of Solomon's reign over Israel, in the month of Ziv, which is the second month, that he began to build the house of the LORD.* (1 Kings 6:1)

Solomon began his reign in 970 BCE, his 4th year was 966 BCE. By adding 480 years to 966 we get 1446 BCE for the date of the Exodus from Egypt. Since the Israelites wandered in the desert for forty years (Numbers 14:34), the date that Joshua and the Israelites began their conquest of the land was 1406 BCE.[7]

There have been several major excavations at the site of Jericho. A good summary can be found by looking at this video *Jericho Found!!*[8]

Archeology at Jericho shows a large fortified city did exist during the Middle Bronze Age and Jericho was destroyed just as described in Joshua.

Here is a quote from Dr. Bryant Wood, Director of Associates for Biblical Research.

"Three major expeditions to the site (i.e. Jericho) over the past 90 years uncovered abundant evidence to support the Biblical account."

The Associates for Biblical Research have a DVD available that clearly shows how Biblical Archaeology is providing solid answers to both defend and promote the truth of God's Word. *The Second Great Battle of Jericho* (DVD), Dr. Bryant Wood, Director of Associates for Biblical Research[9]

NOTES:

1. Enns, Paul P., *Joshua: Bible Study Commentary*, (Grand Rapids, MI: Zondervan, 1961) 58

2. YouTube – Sound of Shofar
https://www.youtube.com/watch?v=1J3tvaVwxIE
Accessed November 17, 2016.

3. *Book of 2 Maccabees* – Written about 123 BCE. 2 Maccabees can be found in the Apocrypha section of the Bible.

4. *Patterns of Evidence - Exodus (DVD)*, produced by Michael Medved, 2015

5. Rohl, David, *From Eden to Exile: The Epic History of the People of the Bible*, (Arrow Books, 2002). 178

6. Rohl, 361

7. Enns, Paul P., *Joshua: Bible Study Commentary,* (Zondervan, 1981), 8-9

8. *Jericho Found!!* Bible Archeology (published 24 Feb, 2013)

Discussion with statements by Dr. Bryant Wood, regarding the Battle at Jericho. Dr. Woods says his findings line up with the description of the biblical account of the destruction of Jericho.
Accessed 19 November 2016
https://www.youtube.com/watch?v=bYrSkikZhxI

9. *Second Great Battle of Jericho*, DVD, 53 minutes
http://www.biblearchaeology.org/bookstore/product.aspx?id=72

Lesson 5: The People

SCRIPTURE:

Achan	Joshua 7:1-26
Rahab	Joshua 2:1-24 and Joshua 6:25
Gibeonites	Joshua 9:1-27
Caleb	Numbers 13:30 and Joshua 14:6-15
Canaanites	Deuteronomy 12:31; 18:9-12

OBJECTIVES:

Learn from choices of others and consequences of those choices.

There is a tendency to think of people as Insiders vs. Outsiders. The stories about individual people in the Book of Joshua show that God not only works with "nations" but with individuals. An "outsider" can benefit by belief in God. An "insider", that uses human understanding, can come to grief.

QUESTIONS:

1. What are lessons from the story of battles at Ai and Achan's action?

2. Why did one man's disobedience cause the whole nation to be defeated?

3. What are lessons from the story of Rahab? Why did she help the spies?

4. What are lessons from the story of the Gibeonites? Discuss the importance of "asking God".

5. Joshua and Calab had been sent out to survey the Land.
When have you stood up against a majority?

6. Who were the Canaanites? What practices were detestable to God?

ADDITIONAL INFORMATION:

About Achan

At the first battle at Ai the Israelites lose. They look to God for an answer. They discover the action by Achan affected the entire nation.

The Israelites were specifically instructed about the destruction of Jericho.

> *"By all means abstain from the accursed things, lest you become accursed when you take of the accursed things, and make the camp of Israel a curse, and trouble it. But all the silver and gold, and vessels of bronze and iron, are consecrated to the LORD; they shall come into the treasury of the LORD."* (Joshua 6:18-19)

> *But the children of Israel committed a trespass regarding the accursed things, for Achan the son of Carmi, the son of Zabdi, the son of Zerah, of the tribe of Judah, took of the accursed things; so the anger of the LORD burned against the children of Israel.* (Joshua 7:1)

Discuss the impact of actions by individuals on people around them, on their community and their world. There are consequences when we take action that is contrary to God's instructions.

About Rahab

Rahab was a Canaanite living in Jericho, but she aided the spies.

Rahab and her family were protected during the battle at Jericho. (Joshua 6:17).

Rahab is found in the genealogy of Jesus:
Rahab was the mother of Boaz,
Boaz married Ruth,
Obed their child was the father of Jesse,
Jesse was the father of King David   (Matthew 1:5-6)

Rahab is listed in Hebrews as a person of faith.

> *"By faith the harlot Rahab did not perish with those who did not believe, when she had received the spies with peace."* (Hebrews 11:31)

About the Gibeonites

The Gibeonites were aware of the Israelites and took action.

Although the Gibeonites lived in Canaan (north of Jerusalem), they tricked Joshua by pretending to have traveled from a far country. They asked to make a covenant with the men of Israel. Because of the covenant, they were allowed to live, but they were made servants to the Israelites.

It is interesting that even though Joshua had been instructed to "destroy all the inhabitants" he allowed the Gibeonites to live because he had made a covenant with them. A covenant was a serious matter, considered as a binding agreement.

Joshua makes a decision based on human observation vs. "ask counsel of the LORD". It is way too easy to be influenced by advice from a friend, advertising, etc. but, are these the best sources of advice?

About Caleb

There were 12 men sent out to explore the land. Only Joshua and Caleb came back with a recommendation to trust God and go ahead.

> *But Joshua the son of Nun and Caleb the son of Jephunneh, who were among those who had spied out the land, tore their clothes; and they spoke to all the congregation of the children of Israel, saying: "The land we passed through to spy out is an exceedingly good land. If the Lord delights in us, then He will bring us into this land and give it to us, 'a land which flows with milk and honey.' Only do not rebel against the Lord, nor fear the people of the land, for they are our bread; their protection has departed from them, and the Lord is with us. Do not fear them." (Numbers 14:6-9)*

Joshua and Caleb were the only ones of their generation that were allowed to enter the Promised Land. (Numbers 14:30)

When the land is divided Caleb is given Hebron. Additional fighting was required to take his inheritance. (Joshua 14:12) Caleb was eighty-five years old when this happened (Joshua 14:10). Warren Wiresbe says "we are never too old to make new conquests of faith in the power of the LORD."[1]

About the Canaanites - Some General Information

The Canaanites were descendants of Noah's son Ham

> *Now the sons of Noah who went out of the ark were Shem, Ham, and Japheth. And Ham was the father of Canaan. (Genesis 9:18)*

> *Canaan begot Sidon his firstborn, and Heth; the Jebusite, the Amorite, and the Girgashite; the Hivite, the Arkite, and the Sinite; the Arvadite, the Zemarite, and the Hamathite. Afterward the families of the Canaanites were dispersed. And the border of the Canaanites was from Sidon as you go toward Gerar, as far as Gaza; then as you go toward Sodom, Gomorrah, Admah, and Zeboiim, as far as Lasha. These were the sons of Ham, according to their families, according to their languages, in their lands and in their nations. (Genesis 10:15-20)*

Practices of the Canaanites

Here is what scripture says about the customs of the Canaanites.

> *When you come into the land which the LORD your God is giving you, you shall not learn to follow the abominations of those nations. There shall not be found among you anyone who makes his son or his daughter pass through the fire, or one who practices witchcraft, or a soothsayer, or one who interprets omens, or a sorcerer, or one who conjures spells, or a medium, or a spiritist, or one who calls up the dead. For all who do these things are an abomination to the LORD, and because of these abominations the LORD your God drives them out from before you. (Deuteronomy 18:9-12)*

According to Paul Enns, there is also archeological evidence about the practices of the Canaanites.

> The Ras Shamra (Ugaritic) tablets reveal the licentious and degrading nature of the Canaanite inhabitants, with their chief emphasis on fertility and sex. Their idolatrous practices of child sacrifice and temple prostitution would have been spiritually contaminating to the Israelites. [2]

NOTES:

1. Wiersbe, Warren W., *Be Strong – Putting God's Power to Work in Your Life,* (David C. Cook, 1993), 125

2. Enns, Paul P., *Joshua: Bible Study Commentary*, (Zondervan, 1981), 10

Lesson 6: The LORD as Divine Warrior

SCRIPTURE:

Joshua 8:1-28   Ai
Joshua 6:2-27   Jericho
Joshua 10:8-14   Gibeon
Joshua 10:40-42   Southern Cities Conquered
Joshua 11:1-23   Northern Cities Conquered

OBJECTIVES:

Gain perspective regarding war and justice. Learn
how God uses war to accomplish his objectives.

SUGGESTED HYMN:

God of our Fathers

QUESTIONS:

1. Why did God order the destruction of the Canaanites?

2. What lessons can you learn from a farmer?

3. How do we reconcile God as loving and also a deity who orders the extermination of whole populations? Is it significant that God defines the area where war is allowed? How does God use war as compared to how humans use war?

4. Were the Israelites any different than the Canaanites?

5. Do you believe in "divine intervention"? Why?

ADDITIONAL INFORMATION:

Why was it necessary to destroy the Canaanites?

The Canaanites were pagans and God wanted to keep His people separate and not influenced by pagan ways: that is worship many gods, sacrifice their children, temple prostitution, etc. (Deuteronomy 12:31 and 18:9-14)

The Canaanites placed their trust in idols, not in the true God.

Lessons from a farmer

Like God providing a special place for the Israelites, a farmer, eliminates the weeds, makes provision for the plants he is caring for.

Think about the activities of a farmer, in many ways this is how God acts.

A farmer acquires a field.

A farmer prepares the land (pulls out the weeds, improves the soil, etc.).

A farmer plants seeds or root cuttings.

A farmer tends the field (pulls out weeds, waters the plants, prunes, etc.).

A farmer uses natural resources (sun, rain, nutrients in the soil, etc.).

A farmer harvests the crop.

It is easy to like the idea that God provides for us and cares for us, we may not be so happy about pruning.

In Scripture, the nation of Israel is sometimes likened to a vine or a vineyard.

> *You have brought a vine out of Egypt; you have cast out the nations, and planted it. You prepared room for it, and caused it to take deep root, and it filled the land.* (Psalm 80:8-9)

Human War vs. God Directed War

Human motives for war are frequently due to aggression or taking action to eliminate a threat.

When God initiates a war one of the characteristics is He may use a small number of people or unusual methods to accomplish the goal.

In the case of the Battle at Jericho, Joshua and the people follow the LORD's unusual instructions.

In the case of the Battle at Gibeon,

> *"the LORD cast down large hailstones from heaven"* (Joshua 10:11)
> and *"the sun stood still"* (Joshua 10:13)

God as Divine Warrior

Here is thoughtful information taken from an article by Peter Kreeft, a professor of philosophy at Boston College and the King's College.[1]

> But is not God compassionate? He is not compassionate to Moloch and Baal and Ashtaroth, and to Canaanites who do their work, who "cause their children to walk through the fire."
>
> "But is not God a lover rather than a warrior? No, God is a lover who is a warrior. The question fails to understand what love is, what the love that God is, is. Love is at war with hate, betrayal, selfishness, and all love's enemies. Love fights. Ask any parent. Yuppie-love, like puppy-love, may be merely "compassion" (the fashionable word today), but father-love and mother-love are war."

Another helpful article can be found in the Introduction to the Anchor Bible Commentary on Joshua by G. Ernest Wright on God as Divine Warrior. Here are a few quotes from his commentary. [2]

> War is a miserable business in a world of men who live in rebellion against the conditions of their creation. Yet God as Suzerain is not defeated. He uses people as they are, to further his own, often mysterious, ends. Hence by implication, we must say that God's use of Israel and her early institution of Holy War does not invest either war or Israel with sanctity or righteousness. On the contrary both are evil; yet God uses Israel as she was for his own purposes. And among the results was the creation of the seedbed of Judaism, Jesus Christ, and the Christian movement.

No one can make any sense out of the biblical attempt to comprehend the role of God in conflict and war when he starts from an idealistic basis in which his own definition of God as love or the Good, as he understands or thinks love and the Good are or should be, in the projected Utopia beyond our current history. Such a basis excludes at the very beginning the mystery and tension between good and evil, love and justice, gospel and law, which form the core of our human experience so that at one and the same time man is a child of nature and a child of God.

It is basically important to understand that in the biblical outlook as a whole the problem of the world is precisely the problem of man.

The biblical manner of making this situation vividly clear is by the use of language and pictures drawn primarily from the ancient world's highest achievement in government, the Suzerain and the empire. The LORDship of God over the world is the first and basic proposition of the Bible. Its corollary is that men, their institutions, nationality, and individuality, find their true freedom and purpose fulfilled only in the Suzerain's service.

The sole guarantee of human freedom is the common recognition that a higher than purely human law is its source and requirement. The freedom of man is protected by the absolute freedom of the Suzerain to preserve it.

God expects humans to know Him. When they worship idols they are without excuse.

For the wrath of God is revealed from heaven against all ungodliness and unrighteousness of men, who suppress the truth in unrighteousness, because what may be known of God is manifest in them, for God has shown it to them. For since the creation of the world His invisible attributes are clearly seen, being understood by the things that are made, even His eternal power and Godhead, so that they are without excuse, because, although they knew God, they did not glorify Him as God, nor were thankful, but became futile in their thoughts, and their foolish hearts were darkened. (Romans 1:18-21)

About the name for God

The word used for God in the book of Joshua is
YAHWEH

In English translations ... the word is LORD.
God first reveals this name to Moses. It is a form
of the Hebrew verb "to be", and signifies that God
defines himself, "*I am who I am.*" (Exodus 3:14)

יהוה

<u>Were the Israelites any different than the Canaanites?</u>

We are all sinners, yet God chooses to use certain people at various times for God's purpose. The Old Testament focus is on obedience. When Israel trusts and is obedient they have God's provision, when they are rebellious they suffer the consequences much as the Canaanites did.

During the time of the Kings, the destruction of Jerusalem is predicted by Isaiah. In this passage Israel is referred to as a vineyard.

> *Now let me sing to my Well-beloved*
> *A song of my Beloved regarding His vineyard:*
> *My Well-beloved has a vineyard*
> *On a very fruitful hill.*
> *He dug it up and cleared out its stones,*
> *And planted it with the choicest vine.*
> *He built a tower in its midst,*
> *And also made a winepress in it;*
> *So He expected it to bring forth good grapes,*
> *But it brought forth wild grapes.*
> (Isaiah 5:1-2)

> *For the vineyard of the LORD of hosts is the house if Israel,*
> *And the men of Judah are His pleasant plant,*
> *He looked for justice, but behold, oppression;*
> *For righteousness, but behold, a cry for help.*
> *(*Isaiah 5:7)

NOTES:

1. Kreeft, Peter, *How to Win the Culture War* (Crisis Magazine, June 1998).
http://www.orthodoxytoday.org/articles/KreetCultureWar.php
Accessed 18 November 2016.

2. Wright, G. Ernest, "Joshua, A New Translation - Introduction and Commentary",
Anchor Bible – Volume 6, (Doubleday, 1982). 27-37

Lesson 7: the Law

SCRIPTURE:

Joshua 8:30-35; 24:1-27
Deuteronomy 30:19-20
Matthew 5:1-7:29

OBJECTIVE:

Understanding the importance of educating people about the Law

Joshua repeatedly reminds the people to follow the Law. The Law includes general ethical principles regulating the relationship between God and humans and between humans. Jesus said *"If you love Me, keep My commandments."* (John 14:15)

QUESTIONS:

1. What is the difference between God's Laws vs. human laws? Can you give an example?

2. Why are choices important? What is meant by "choose life"? (Deuteronomy 30:19)

3. List some of the important laws found in the Bible. Are these instructions familiar? Discuss benefits of following these laws.

4. What laws do you observe? Who's laws?

ADDITIONAL INFORMATION:

God's Laws and human laws

Law, in a generic sense, is a body of rules of action or conduct prescribed by a controlling authority.

Although many laws in today's world (human laws) are consistent with God's Laws, there are others that are in direct conflict with the Laws of God. It is important to distinguish between God's laws and human laws.

Natural Law and Common Law

One guideline that humans use is called Natural Law. Natural Law refers to the use of reason to analyze both social and personal human nature to deduce binding rules of moral behavior.

An advocate of natural moral law believes that there are certain moral laws or norms that are true and can be discerned by all people.

Common law was a legal system that grew out of court decisions based on religious principles.[1] There are two fundamental laws on which all major religions and philosophies agree: Do all you have agreed to do, and do not encroach on other persons or their property. These rules are the basis of common law.[2]

Ruler's Law

Throughout most of history man has lived under what could be called Ruler's laws. The laws are made by those in authority and the power to enforce the laws rests in the government.

These laws may include giving special privileges to certain groups of people, defining who has to pay taxes, who can hold property, etc. Many laws are only based on custom and may change over time or are different in different places. For example, Americans are expected to drive on the right side of the road while people in Britain drive on the left side of the road.

About Choices

When you need to make choices, where do you turn to for advice?

Here Moses speaks to the children of Israel in the land of Moab after 40 years in the wilderness.

> *I call heaven and earth as witnesses today against you, that I have set before you life and death, blessing and cursing; therefore **choose life**, that both you and your descendants may live; that you may love the LORD your God, that you may obey His voice, and that you may cling to Him, for he is your life and the length of your days; and that you may dwell in the land which the LORD swore to your fathers, to Abraham, Isaac, and Jacob, to give them"* (Deuteronomy 30:19-20)

Joshua challenges his people to choose.

> *And if it seems evil to you to serve the LORD, choose for yourselves this day whom you will serve, whether the gods which your fathers served that were on the other side of the River, or the gods of the Amorites, in whose land you dwell. But as for me and my house, we will serve the LORD."* (Joshua 24:15)

Benefits of Knowing the Law

Some of the most important laws we need to observe are not observed in order to avoid punishment, but to live.

Advice from Joshua

Joshua's life is a model of God directed leadership. Joshua places great importance on the study and observance of the law.

> *This Book of the Law shall not depart from your mouth, but you shall meditate in it day and night, that you may observe to do according to all that is written in it. For then you will make your way prosperous, and then you will have good success.* (Joshua 1:8)

> *And afterward he read all the words of the law, the blessings and the cursings, according to all that is written in the Book of the Law. There was not a word of all that Moses had commanded which Joshua did not read before all the assembly of Israel, with the women, the little ones, and the strangers who were living among them.* (Joshua 8:34-35)

Role of the Holy Spirit, The New Covenant

The Old Testament places a lot of importance on obedience. The New Testament tells us that humans, by their own effort, are unable to meet the requirements of The Law. The New Testament also tells us that by God's Grace, Jesus died for our sins. God gives us the gift of faith to believe in Him and also gives us the Holy Spirit to guide and direct us. We find the promise of this in Jeremiah and Ezekiel.

> *But this is the covenant that I will make with the house of Israel after those days, says the LORD: I will put My law in their minds, and write it on their hearts; and I will be their God, and they shall be My people.* (Jeremiah 31:33)

> *"I will give you a new heart and put a new spirit within you; I will take the heart of stone out of your flesh and give you a heart of flesh. I will put My Spirit within you and cause you to walk in My statutes, and you will keep My judgments and do them."* (Ezekiel 36:26-27)

Without the Holy Spirit we are unable to keep God's commandments.

> Jesus tells us, *"If you love Me, keep my commandment. And I will pray the Father, and He will give you another Helper, that He may abide with you forever - The Spirit of truth, whom the world cannot receive, because it neither sees Him nor knows Him; but you know Him, for He dwells with you and will be in you."* (John 14:15-17)

> *But the Helper, the Holy Spirit, whom the Father will send in My name, He will teach you all things, and bring to your remembrance all things that I said to you.* (John 14:26)

Peter (one of the 12 disciples of Jesus) to the crowd after healing a lame man:

> *"Repent therefore and be converted, that your sins may be blotted out, so that times of refreshing may come from the presence of the Lord, "* (Acts 3:19)

Peter addressing the crowd at Pentecost:

> *Then Peter said to them, "Repent, and let every one of you be baptized in the name of Jesus Christ for the remission of sins; and you shall receive the gift of the Holy Spirit. For the promise is to you and to your children, and to all who are afar off, as many as the LORD our God will call."* (Acts 2:38-39)

> Paul tells us in his letter to the Galatians, *"So I say, live by the Spirit, and you will not gratify the desires of the sinful nature."* (Galatians 5:16)

Why study God's Laws
===

For those who have not studied the Law, a sampling (both Old Testament and New Testament) is included in this study to acquaint you with the wealth of guidance that is available.

By using prayer and the help of the Holy Spirit, the importance of these laws and guidelines will become apparent.

Although many Christians today seem to think that they no longer need to study the Law. *Jesus Christ has set Christian free, but we still have the choice to sin or not to sin.* [3]

Also, Jesus in his teaching made it clear how we should live.

Here are some comments by Nicky Gumbel about what he calls the Jesus Lifestyle based on the Sermon on the Mount. (Matthew 5:1-7:29)

> "Jesus was not laying down a new law to replace the Old Covenant of Moses; He was teaching His followers how to live out the Jesus Lifestyle. Many who would not call themselves Christians claim to live by the teaching of Jesus in the Sermon on the Mount. If they had really read it carefully they would see that it is quite impossible even to begin to live as Jesus taught without the help of His Spirit.
>
> Perhaps that was one of the purposes of the sermon. The Reformers in the sixteenth century used to say that the law sends us to Christ to be justified and Christ sends us back to the law to be sanctified. Reading the Sermon on the Mount should make those who do not know Christ, and indeed all of us, cry out for mercy and help. As we receive Christ and the help of His Spirit, He sends us back to the Sermon on the Mount to learn how to live out our faith. Jesus is teaching us here how to work out what God has worked in." [4]

Here is some advice from John Calvin about the benefit of studying the law.

> Regarding the proper purpose of the law. "Here is the best instrument for them to learn more thoroughly each day the nature of the Lord's will to which they aspire, and to confirm them in the understanding of it. It is as if some servant, already prepared with all earnestness of heart to commend himself to his master, must search out and observe his master's ways more carefully in order to conform and accommodate himself to them. And not one of us may escape from this necessity. For no man has heretofore attained to such wisdom as to be unable, from the daily instruction of the law, to make fresh progress toward a purer knowledge of the divine will." [5]

About God's Laws

The law of God given to Moses are recorded in the first five books of the Bible (Genesis, Exodus, Leviticus, Numbers and Deuteronomy). Besides the Ten Commandment there are various laws about what to do and what to refrain from doing.

A frequent way used to divide these laws are as follows:

Moral Law

The value of these laws is considered obvious by reason and common sense. The moral law includes regulation on justice, respect, and sexual conduct and includes the Ten Commandments.

Ceremonial Law

These laws are not obvious to common sense; for example, the need for sacrifice and rejection of certain foods. They include laws about sacrifice, feasts and festivals, importance of the Sabbath, etc.

Judicial/Civil Law

These laws include everything from murder to restitution for a man gored by an ox. (Exodus 21:28-32)

According to Paul:

> *"All Scripture is given by inspiration of God, and is profitable for doctrine, for reproof, for correction, for instruction in righteousness, that the man of God may be complete, thoroughly equipped for every good work. (2 Timothy 3:16-17)*

The 10 Commandments

The Ten Commandments, written on stone tablets by the hand of God, are found in Exodus 20:1-17 and Deuteronomy 5:6-22.

And God spoke all these words, saying: "I am the LORD your God, who brought you out of the land of Egypt, out of the house of bondage.

(1) "You shall have no other gods before Me.

(2) "You shall not make for yourself a carved image — any likeness of anything that is in heaven above, or that is in the earth beneath, or that is in the water under the earth; you shall not bow down to them nor serve them. For I, the LORD your God, am a jealous God, visiting the iniquity of the fathers upon the children to the third and fourth generations of those who hate Me, but showing mercy to thousands, to those who love Me and keep My commandments.

(3) "You shall not take the name of the LORD your God in vain, for the LORD will not hold him guiltless who takes His name in vain.

(4) "Remember the Sabbath day, to keep it holy. Six days you shall labor and do all your work, but the seventh day is the Sabbath of the LORD your God. In it you shall do no work: you, nor your son, nor your daughter, nor your male servant, nor your female servant, nor your cattle, nor your stranger who is within your gates. For in six days the LORD made the heavens and the earth, the sea, and all that is in them, and rested the seventh day. Therefore the LORD blessed the Sabbath day and hallowed it.

(5) "Honor your father and your mother, that your days may be long upon the land which the LORD your God is giving you.

(6) "You shall not murder.

(7) "You shall not commit adultery.

(8) "You shall not steal.

(9) "You shall not bear false witness against your neighbor.

(10) "You shall not covet your neighbor's house; you shall not covet your neighbor's wife, nor his male servant, nor his female servant, nor his ox, nor his donkey, nor anything that is your neighbor's."

Other Laws and Regulations given from God to the Israelite people via Moses (Deuteronomy 4:13-14) - also found in Exodus, Leviticus, and Numbers.

The Law is recorded in the first five books of the Bible. During the Exodus, Moses received ten laws direct from God at Mt. Sinai. The Book of Joshua is very specific regarding the importance of the Israelite nation following The Law. The story of Achan highlights how even one person can impact the whole nation. Transgression of the law was viewed as an offense not only to society (civil law) but also against God.

Moral laws - about murder, theft, honesty, adultery, etc.

Example: *"You shall not steal, nor deal falsely, nor lie to one another"*
          (Leviticus 19:11)

Example: 'You shall do no injustice in judgment, in measurement of length, weight, or volume. You shall have honest scales, honest weights, an honest ephah, and an honest hin: (Leviticus 19:35)

Social laws - About property, justice, inheritance, marriage and divorce, etc.

Example: *"You shall appoint judges and officers in all your gates, which the LORD your God gives you, according to your tribes, and they shall judge the people with just judgement. You shall not pervert justice; you shall not show partiality, nor take a bribe, for a bribe blinds the eyes of the wise and twists the words of the righteous."* (Deuteronomy 16:18-19)

Example: Nor shall you make marriages with them. You shall not give your daughter to their son, nor take their daughter for your son. For they will turn your sons away from following Me, to serve other gods; (Deuteronomy 7:3-4)

Purity & Dietary laws – About clean and unclean things, on cooking and storing food

Example: there are many statutes about food, these guidelines are still useful to follow for better health

Tithes, Sacrifices, Offerings

A tithe was understood as 10% of your income and was used to support the Levites who were responsible for various religious duties.

Example: *"You shall truly tithe all the increase of your grain that the field produces year by year"* (Deuteronomy 14:22)

Feasts

Passover is a significant yearly celebration for Jewish people. The general principal of celebrating significant events is still important today as we celebrate the birth of Jesus at Christmas, the death and resurrection of Jesus at Easter, and the arrival of the Holy Spirit at Pentecost.

Other Laws and Guidelines from the Old Testament

In addition to the Laws found in the first 5 books of the Bible (The Torah), guidelines can be found throughout the Old Testament. Sometimes the guidelines are taught as the Bible describes events in history. Sometimes the guidelines are stated as advice, many are found in Psalms and Proverbs.

Psalms

But his delight is in the law of the LORD, and in His law he meditates day and night. (Psalms 1:2)

Proverbs

For whom the LORD loves He corrects, just as a father the son in whom he delights. (Proverbs 3:12)

Trust in the LORD with all your heart, and lean not on your own understanding; in all your ways acknowledge Him, And He shall direct your paths. (Proverbs 3:5-6)

A soft answer turns away wrath, but a harsh word stirs up anger. (Proverbs 15:1)

Pride goes before destruction, and a haughty spirit before a fall. (Proverbs 16:18)

Do not withhold good from those to whom it is due, when it is in the power of your hand to do so. (Proverbs 3:27)

Teaching by Jesus about the Law

Joshua clearly thought it was important to study the Law. For us today we have additional instructions in the New Testament. Both Jesus and the Apostles had a lot to say about the role of the Law.

> *Jesus said to him, "'You shall love the LORD your God with all your heart, with all your soul, and with all your mind.' This is the first and great commandment. And the second is like it: 'You shall love your neighbor as yourself.' On these two commandments hang all the Law and the Prophets."* (Matthew 22:37-40)

> *"Do not think that I came to destroy the Law or the Prophets. I did not come to destroy but to fulfill.* (Matthew 5:17)

> *Let your light so shine before men, that they may see your good works and glorify your Father in heaven.* (Matthew 5:16)

> *"For if you forgive men their trespasses, your heavenly Father will also forgive you.* (Matthew 6:14)

> *"Do not lay up for yourselves treasures on earth, where moth and rust destroy and where thieves break in and steal; but lay up for yourselves treasures in heaven, where neither moth nor rust destroys and where thieves do not break in and steal. For where your treasure is, there your heart will be also.* (Matthew 6:19-21)

> *But let your 'Yes' be 'Yes,' and your 'No,' 'No.' for whatever is more than these is from the evil one.* (Matthew 5:37)

> *"Therefore whoever hears these sayings of Mine, and does them, I will liken him to a wise man who built his house on the rock: and the rain descended, the floods came, and the winds blew and beat on that house; and it did not fall, for it was founded on the rock.* (Matthew 7:24-25)

> *"Judge not, and you shall not be judged. Condemn not, and you shall not be condemned. Forgive, and you will be forgiven.* (Luke 6:37)

> *"If you love Me, keep My commandments.* (John 14:15)

> *And remember the words of the Lord Jesus, that He said, 'It is more blessed to give than to receive.'* (Acts 20:35b)

Teaching by Paul about the Law

Paul was a missionary apostle mainly to Gentiles. His journeys, sufferings, words and works are described in the Acts of the Apostles and in letters which he wrote to the churches at Rome, Corinth, and other places.

For not the hearers of the law are just in the sight of God, but the doers of the law will be justified. (Romans 2:13)

I beseech you therefore, brethren, by the mercies of God, that you present your bodies a living sacrifice, holy, acceptable to God, which is your reasonable service. And do not be conformed to this world, but be transformed by the renewing of your mind, that you may prove what is that good and acceptable and perfect will of God. (Romans 12:1-2)

Regarding generosity, Christians are encouraged to give offerings to support their Church and to help the poor and needy.

But this I say: He who sows sparingly will also reap sparingly, and he who sows bountifully will also reap bountifully. So let each one give as he purposes in his heart, not grudgingly or of necessity; for God loves a cheerful giver. (2 Corinthians 9:6-7)

Let him who stole steal no longer, but rather let him labor, working with his hands what is good, that he may have something to give him who has need. (Ephesians 4:28)

Let all bitterness, wrath, anger, clamor, and evil speaking be put away from you, with all malice. And be kind to one another, tenderhearted, forgiving one another, just as God in Christ forgave you. (Ephesians 4:31-32)

Finally, my brethren, be strong in the LORD and in the power of His might. Put on the whole armor of God, that you may be able to stand against the wiles of the devil. (Ephesians 6:10-20)

Do not be anxious about anything, but in everything, by prayer and petition, with thanksgiving present your requests to God." (Philippians 4:6)

Finally, brethren, whatever things are true, whatever things are noble, whatever things are just, whatever things are pure, whatever things are lovely, whatever things are of good report, if there is any virtue and if there is anything praiseworthy – meditate on these things. (Philippians 4:8)

And whatever you do, do it heartily, as to the LORD and not to men. (Colossians 3:23)

NOTES:

1. Mayberry, Richard J., *Whatever Happened to Justice?* (Bluestocking Press, 1993), 30

2. Mayberry, 35

3. Sproul, R. C., *Chosen by God*, (Tyndale, 1986), 49

4. Gumbel, Nicky. The Jesus Lifestyle, (Alpha, 2010), 11

5. Calvin, John. *Calvin: Institutes of the Christian Religion – Volume 1,* edited by John T. McNeill, translated by Ford Lewis Battles, (The Westminster Press, 1960), 360

Lesson 8: The Land is Divided, Unfinished Business

SCRIPTURE:

Genesis 12:2-3
Deuteronomy 4:5-8
Joshua 14:1 – 21:45

OBJECTIVE:

Understand the LORD's provision for organizing society.

The conquest takes about 7 years. Many years later, Joshua divided the land based on God's direction. Some tribes are allocated land where additional battles are necessary. During the following years prior to the establishment of the monarchy there is some success and lots of failure (see the Book of Judges).

As you look at the detailed instructions in Joshua 14:1 – 21:45, try to see the various principles that are present: the division of the land, the importance of worship, the role of the priests, the provision for avoiding unnecessary violence and revenge.

QUESTIONS:

1. Discuss the plan to distribute the land.
   What was done, for what purpose?
   What are the benefits of giving each tribe a specific area?

2. The Israelites were given a special mission. In what ways have they obeyed this instruction?

3. There are consequences of partial implementation.

Why is it usually the case that disobedience to God is a gradual thing?
What does it take to stay true to the LORD?
What happens when we backslide?
How can we keep from making compromises like the Israelites did after the conquest?

ADDITIONAL INFORMATION:

God's Instructions

Each tribe is given specific land based on the original guidelines established by God.

A central point of worship was established near Shechem at Shiloh.

With Israel's settlement in the land, a permanent location for the tabernacle became essential. The initial site of Shiloh, meaning "place of rest," was located in the central hill country of Ephraim, just south of Shechem and Mount Gerizim.[1]

The Priests (Levites) were not given a separate area of land but were given specific towns and pasture lands for their flocks (Joshua 21:1-42).

There was a distinct purpose in scattering the Levites throughout the land in the forty-eight towns. The Levites were to instruct the people; this was God's unique methodology for ensuring the dissemination of the Word of God throughout the land." [2]

Six Cities of Refuge were established. (Joshua 20:1-9)

> Kedesh in Galilee in the hill country of Naphtali
> Shechem in the hill country of Ephraim
> Kiriath Arba (Hebron) in the hill country of Judah.
> Bezer on the east side of the Jordan in the tribe of Reuben
> Ramoth in Gilead in the tribe of Gad
> Golan in Bashan in the tribe of Manasseh
>
> *"that whoever killed a person accidentally might flee there, and not die by the hand of the avenger of blood until he stood before the congregation."* (Joshua 20:9)

Killing an innocent person was considered a terrible offense. Willful murder demanded the death penalty. Provision was made if someone killed another accidently.[3]

Laws were given by God to the Israelites including the importance of worship, protection of property and restitution, social responsibilities, etc., provisions for judges to *"judge the people with just judgement"* (Deuteronomy 16:18-20)

Did the Israelites ever completely take possession of the land?

Almost 600 years after Joshua and the Israelites enter the Land, David captures Jerusalem. (2 Samuel Chapter 5:6-10)

During the reign of King Solomon, the extent of land controlled was similar to the Promised Land, however the vision of a kingdom under God is still to be realized.

The special mission of the Israelites

"We must never forget that God put Israel in the world to be the channel for His blessing, which involves, among other things, the writing of the Scriptures and the coming of the Savior"[4]

"The emergence of a universal family in God still waits to come true in history".[5]

From the LORD to Abraham
"...And in you all the families of the earth shall be blessed." (Genesis 12:3)

From the LORD to Isaac

"And I will make your descendants multiply as the stars of heaven; I will give to your descendants all these lands; and in your seed all the nations of the earth shall be blessed; because Abraham obeyed My voice and kept My charge, My commandments, My statutes, and My laws." (Genesis 26:4)

From the LORD to Jacob

"And behold, the LORD stood above it and said: "I am the LORD God of Abraham your father and the God of Isaac; the land on which you lie I will give to you and your descendants. Also your descendants shall be as the dust of the earth; you shall spread abroad to the west and the east, to the north and the south; and in you and in your seed all the families of the earth shall be blessed. Behold, I am with you and will keep you wherever you go, and will bring you back to this land; for I will not leave you until I have done what I have spoken to you? (Genesis 28:13-15)

From Moses to the Israelites:

And what great nation is there that has such statutes and righteous judgments as are in all this law which I set before you this day." (Deuteronomy 4:8)

Unfinished Business

These are the nations the LORD left: the five rulers of the Philistines, all the Canaanites, the Sidonians, and the Hivites living in the Lebanon Mountains from Mount Baal Hermon to Lebo Hamath. The Israelites lived among the Canaanites, Hittitles, Amorites, Perizzites, Hivites and Jebusites.

> *"Thus the children of Israel dwelt among the Canaanites, the Hittites, the Amorites, the Perizzites, the Hivites, and the Jebusites. And they took their daughters to be their wives, and gave their daughters to their sons; and they served their gods."* (Judges 3:5-6)

The book of Judges tells of what happened to the Israelites after Joshua's time.

> After Joshua died, *"Then the children of Israel did evil in the sight of the LORD, and served the Baals; and they forsook the LORD God of their fathers, who had brought them out of the land of Egypt; and they followed other gods from among the gods of the people who were all around them, and they bowed down to them; and they provoked the LORD to anger. They forsook the LORD and served Baal and the Ashtoreths."* (Judges 2:11-13)

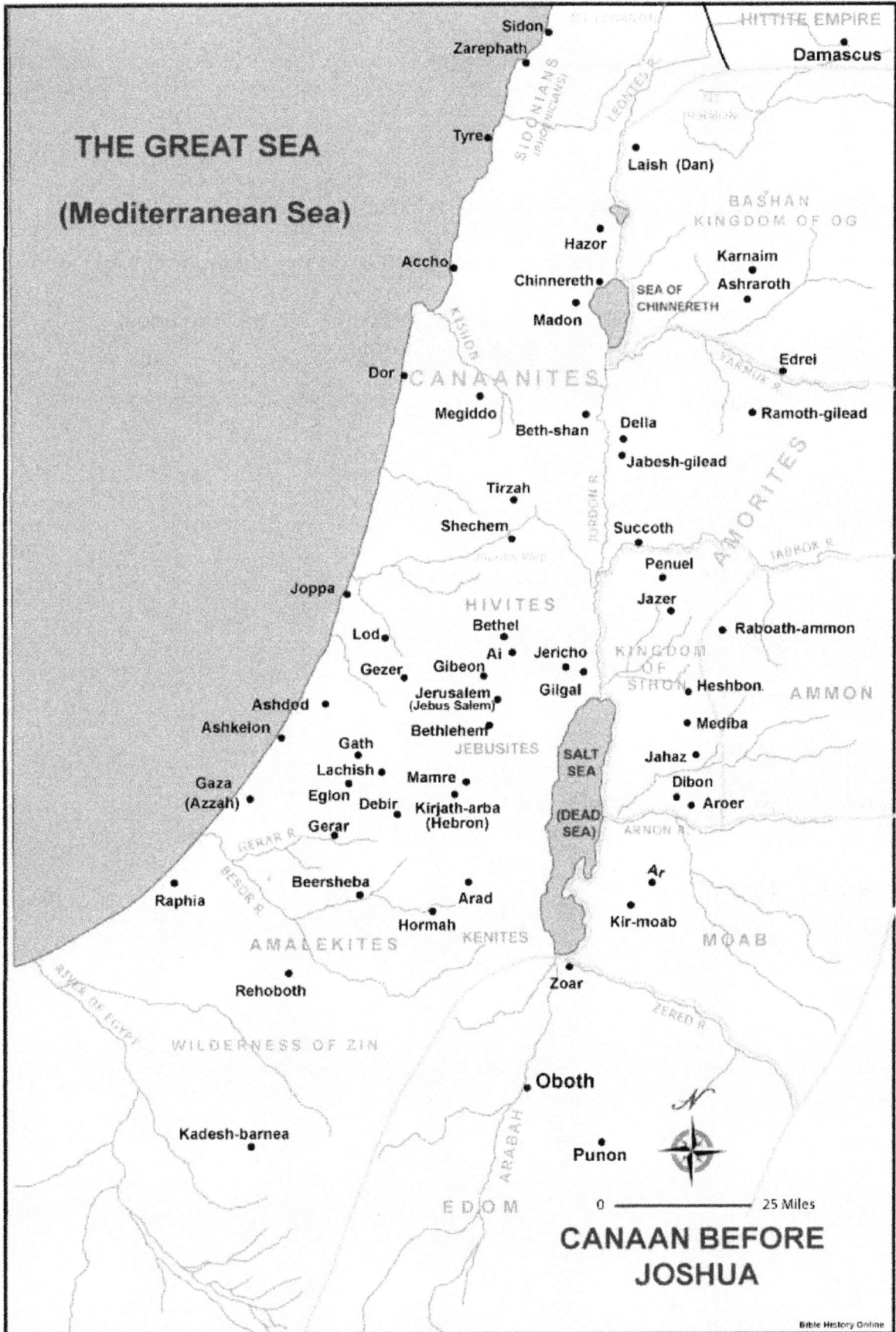

THE GREAT SEA

(Mediterranean Sea)

CANAAN BEFORE JOSHUA

Bible History Online

0 ———— 25 Miles

About the Tribes of Israel (Joshua 14:1 – 19:51)

Sons of Jacob	Mother	Land Allocated
Ruben	Leah	east of the Jordan River
Simeon	Leah	Cities in land allocated to Judah (Joshua 19:1-9)
Levi	Leah	No land, but towns to live in with pasturelands for their flocks and herds
Judah	Leah	
Dan	Bilhah	
Naphtali	Bilhah	
Gad	Zillpah	east of the Jordan River
Asher	Zilpah	
Issachar	Leah	
Zebulun	Leah	
Joseph	Rachel	land given to two sons: Manasseh and Ephraim
Benjamin	Rachel	

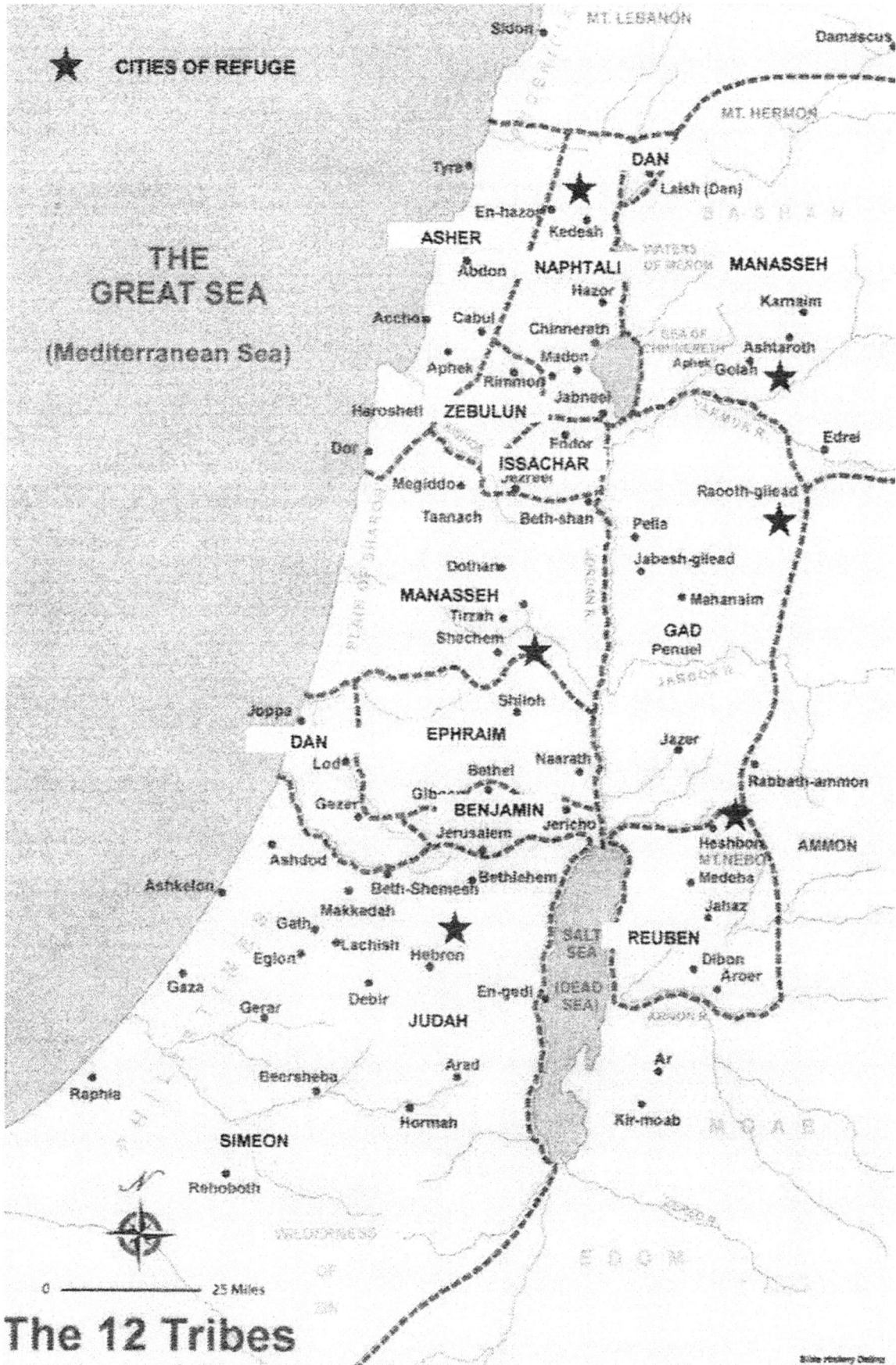

The 12 Tribes

NOTES:

1. Enns, Paul P., *Joshua: Bible Study Commentary.* (Zondervan, 1981), 121

2. Enns, 128

3. Navigators, *A Life-changing encounter with God's Word from the book of Joshua,* (NavPress, 2013), 131-132

4. Wiersbe, Warren W., *Be Strong – Putting God's Power to Work in Your Life,* (David C. Cook, 1993), 80

5. Bowie, Walter Russell., "The Book of Genesis" – Exposition, *The Interpreter's Bible, Volume 1,* (Abingdon Press, 1953), 575

Lesson 9: The Land

SCRIPTURE:
  Joshua 1:1-7

OBJECTIVE:

Learn if the promise of land to the Israelites is still relevant today.

QUESTIONS:

1. Was the Land promised? Is the promise still in effect?

Difference between land "given" and land "possessed".

Whose land: God's land or whoever is the occupier?
Is there something special about this particular land?

2. What are some of the names for The Land?

3. What do you know about the modern state of Israel?

4. What does it mean to be a Palestinian?

5. Why are the Jewish people still a distinct ethnic group today? What factors have kept their culture alive?

6. Is there something special about this particular land? Why? What is special about Jerusalem?

ADDITIONAL INFORMATION:

God's Land

It's helpful to acknowledge who is in charge, *"the earth is the LORD's."* (Psalm 24:1) We are expected to be stewards. God is the landlord.

> *"I will put My Spirit in you, and you shall live, and I will place you in your own land. Then you shall know that I, the LORD, have spoken it and performed it," says the LORD. (*Ezekiel 37:14)

Names for The Land

Levant – A French word meaning "the Orient", used by archeologists and historians to describe the geographical region defined by natural frontiers, encompassing the eastern shores of the Mediterranean Sea from roughly the Isthmus of Suez to the Taurus Mountains, including present day Israel, Lebanon, western Jordan, the Sinai in Egypt and that part of Syria defined by the Orontes River Valley and the region of Aleppo.

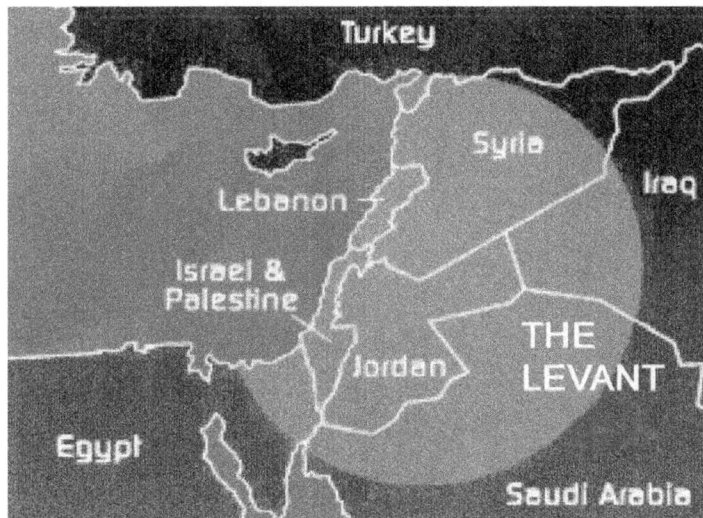

Palestine - The term "Palestine" is not found in the Bible. The term Palestine originated with the Greek word *Philistia*, referring to the southeastern coast of the Mediterranean Sea, where the Philistines once lived. Under Roman rule in the second century CE, the name was changed to Palestine.

British Mandate of Palestine - After the First World War and formally approved by the League of Nations in 1922 - included what today is Israel and Jordan.

Holy Land - Land considered holy by Jews, Christians and Muslims. Significant in Christianity because it is the place of birth, ministry, crucifixion and resurrection of Jesus. Also the term used for the land during the Crusades in the Middle Ages.

Land of Canaan - Also referred to as the land of the Canaanites, Hittites, Hivites, Perizzites, Girgashites, Amorites and Jebusites. (Joshua 3:10)

Promised Land - The land promised to Abraham (Isaac and Jacob) by God. (Genesis 17:7-11; Joshua 1:1-7)

Land east of Jordan - allocated to the tribes of Reuben, Gad and Manasseh

> *Then Moses commanded the children of Israel, saying: "This is the land which you shall inherit by lot, which the LORD has commanded to give to the nine tribes and to the half-tribe. For the tribe of the children of Reuben according to the house of their fathers, and the tribe of the children of Gad according to the house of their fathers, have received their inheritance; and the half-tribe of Manasseh has received its inheritance. The two tribes and the half-tribe have received their inheritance on this side of the Jordan, across from Jericho eastward, toward the sunrise.* (Numbers 34:13-15)

Land of Israel
Israelite kingdoms and states existed intermittently in the region for over a millennium, with Jerusalem as their capital.

Saul's Kingdom 1020 to 1000 BCE

David's Kingdom 1000 to 961 BCE

Solomon's Kingdom 961 to 931 BCE

Kingdom of Israel 931 BCE to 722 BCE (Northern Kingdom)

Kingdom of Judah 931 BCE to 586 BCE (Southern Kingdom)

Maccabean Kingdom of Judah 143 BCE to 63 BCE
(Conquered by Pompey in 63 BCE)

Description of the land about 1922 prior to return of the Jews

> Before the arrival of the Jews, Arab *fellahin* (peasants) stood next to the Chinese coolies on the lower rungs of the world's income ladder, working for a pittance from morning til night for the *effendis* (landholders) who owned most of the land. Of the 650,000 Arabs in Palestine in 1922, over 100,000 were desert nomads, and the rest, with the exception of the small class of *effendis*, were landless peasants who lived no better than European serfs at the time of the Crusades. The *fellahin* burned camel dung for fuel, slept in the same huts with their animals, faced a life-expectancy of thirty-five years, and, until death came, had no hope for a better future. [1]

About the modern state of Israel:

In 1917 Lord Balfour, the British Foreign Secretary stated "His Majesty's Government view with favor the establishment in Palestine of a national home of the Jewish people." World events and the needs of the Zionists ...fostered five waves of immigration to Palestine.

In 1880 - 1900 came the tillers of the soil

1900-1914 came scientific farmers and laborers to build the country's agriculture

1918 - 1924 young people, entrepreneurs, speculators to build cities, found industries, to organize an army and establish educational institutions.

1924-1939 came the intellectuals, professionals and bureaucrats to draw blueprints for democracy and statehood.

after World War II, Jews came from every walk of life.[2]

In 1947 the UN voted to partition western Palestine into a Jewish and an Arab state and establish Jerusalem as an international zone. The Jewish leadership in Palestine accepted this plan. The Arabs not only rejected the UN Partition Plan but attacked Israel from all sides. There are various explanations on why some Arabs left their homes.

"Had these leaders, (the Palestinian Arab leaders) and their counterparts in the neighboring Arab states, accepted the UN resolution, there would have been no war and no dislocation in the first place."[3]

The modern state of Israel came into existence on May 14, 1948.[4]

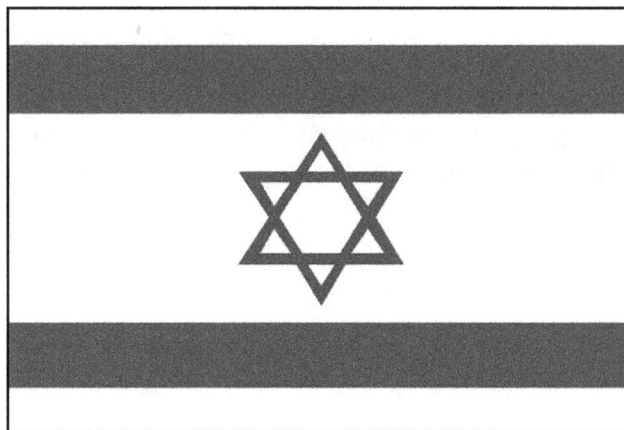

On the day Israel declared its independence, the Arab League Secretary, General Azzam Pasha declared jihad, a holy war. He said, "This will be a war of extermination and a momentous massacre". In 1949, Israel agreed to armistice in separate agreements with Egypt, Syria, Lebanon and Jordan.

In 1956, Arab nations attacked Israel (the Sinai War). Egyptian president Nasser announced that he would destroy the Israeli state. Israel defended itself and captured Sinai and Gaza. Due to international involvement, Sinai and Gaza were returned to the Egyptians.

In 1967, Arab nations (Egypt, Jordan, and Syria) attacked Israel (Six Day War) - Israel defended itself and as a result acquired the West Bank, the Golan Heights, East Jerusalem, Gaza and the Sinai Peninsula up to the Suez Canal.

In 1973, Egypt and Syria attacked Israel (Yom Kippur War), Israel defended itself.

In 1979, the Egypt-Israel Peace treaty was signed by Egyptian president, Anwar Sadat and Israeli prime minister Menachem Begin.
The main features of the treaty were mutual recognition, cessation of the state of war that had existed since the 1948 Arab-Israeli war, normalization of relations and the complete withdrawal by Israel of its armed forces and civilians from the Sinai Peninsula which Israel had captured during the Six-day War in 1967. [5]

Several attempts have been made at conflict resolution, no resolution as of 2019.

Israel Population (2011)[6]

Ethnicity		Religious Affiliation	
Jewish	75.4 %	Jewish	75.4 %
Arab	20.6 %	Muslim	16.9 %
Other	4.1 %	Christian	2.1 %
		Druze	1.7 %
		Other	4.0 %

A Gallup survey in 2015 determined that 65% of Israelis say they are either "not religious" or "convinced atheists", while 30 % say they are "religious".

The People Living in the Land - Some Definitions

Palestinians
Name given to people living in Palestine...Arabs, Jews, Christians, Druze, others. There was a small population in the area prior to the immigration of Jewish people beginning in 1918.

As the economy grew Arabs seeking employment moved to the region from Egypt, Syria, Lebanon and other Arab countries. By 1930 the trend toward higher living and health standards for the Palestinian Arabs was well established. Per Mikhael in the Horizons Study[7], *the number of "indigenous" Palestinians who fled their homes in 1948 was 750,000.* If "indigenous" means original inhabitants (i.e. the Canaanites, etc.) then the number is 0.

Palestine
Name given to an area governed by the Romans, the name continued to be used through subsequent rulers (Persians, Turks, Christians/Crusaders, Mameluks, Ottoman Turks, Britain).

The idea of Palestine as a "nation" is a recent development (example the Kurds are a nation but not a state). Formation of states as a result of decolonization in Africa and Asia occurred only after World War II. There is no language known as Palestinian, no Palestinian culture distinct from other Arabs in the area. In 1921, Palestine included both Palestine and Jordan.

Jews
People with Jewish ancestry
People converted to Judaism
People who practice Judaism: Orthodox, Conservative, Reformed, etc.

Israel
Name given by God to Jacob, son of Isaac, & grandson of Abraham (Genesis 35:9)
The Biblical land of the Israelites
Northern kingdom during the period of the Divided Kingdom
The modern state of Israel that has existed since 1948

Israeli
People living in Israel, something from or related to Israel

Hebrew
Name used for Jews who use the Hebrew language
Descriptor for converts, from Judaism, example: Hebrew Christians
Descendants of Abraham, Isaac and Jacob (Abraham was a descendent of Shem, one of Noah's sons)

Druze
A separate ethnic group in Israel. Their culture is Arab and their language is Arabic. They support Israel and serve in the Israeli military.

Arabs

Descendants of Abraham's son Ishmael (Genesis 17:20)

Before the spread of Islam, Arab referred to any of the largely Semitic people from the northern and central Arabian Peninsula.

In modern usage, a heterogeneous collection of Arabic-speaking peoples in the Arab world.

Christians

Not a specific ethnic group but people that adhere to Christianity, an Abrahamic, Monotheistic religion based on the life and teachings of Jesus Christ.

Muslims

People that follow the religion of Islam.

Source from most of the above information is from Wikipedia

Where are the Jews today?

The Kingdom was divided in 931 BCE. Then in 722 BCE, the tribes in the Northern Kingdom of Israel were conquered by Assyrians and deported. In 586 BCE, the people in the Southern Kingdom of Judah were deported to Babylon.

When Babylon captured Jerusalem many Jews were deported to Babylon. During the reign of Cyrus (539 BCE), the Jews were allowed to return to Jerusalem, but many stayed in Babylonia. (Ezra 1:1-4) Until recently, there were many Jewish communities in Iraq and Iran.

During the first century CE, about a million Jews were living in Egypt. Jews were also living in Rome, Greece and Asia Minor.

After the fall of Judea in 70 CE the Jews were scattered to many lands. Many successfully retained their language, customs and culture. The Hebrew language ceased to be an everyday spoken language somewhere between 200 and 400 CE. Then in the 19th century, Hebrew was revived as a spoken and literary language. Modern Hebrew is one of the two official languages of Israel (the other being Arabic).

During the middle Ages, two main branches of modern Judaism originated: the Ashkenazim (in France and Germany) and the Sephardim (in Spain and the Mediterranean).

Some Jews continued to live in Israel, however, beginning in the late 1800's, Jews began to return to Israel.

Jews came from many lands.... from Yemen and Germany, Morocco and Russia, Turkey and Poland, Ethiopia and Iraq, Egypt and Syria[8]

Out of 14.3 million Jewish people in the world, 43% reside in Israel.[9]

What activities keep a culture alive?

Ethnicity refers to cultural factors, including nationality, regional culture, ancestry, and language. In the case of the Jews some of the factors that have kept them as a distinct ethnic group are the following:

The tradition of keeping separate (avoid intermarriage)
The tradition of passing on their customs and laws
  The celebration of the Passover
  Observing Dietary Laws
  Circumcision
  Observance of the Sabbath
  Importance of family

About "The Jews" by Mark Twain[10]

To conclude. - If the statistics are right, the Jews constitute but one per cent of the human race. It suggests a nebulous dim puff of star-dust lost in the blaze of the Milky Way. Properly the Jew ought hardly to be heard of; but he is heard of, has always been heard of. He is as prominent on the planet as any other people, and his commercial importance is extravagantly out of proportion to the smallness of his bulk. His contributions to the world's list of great names in literature, science, art, music, finance, medicine, and abstruse learning are also away out of proportion to the weakness of his numbers.

He has made a marvelous fight in this world, in all the ages; and has done it with his hands tied behind him. He could be vain of himself, and be excused for it. The Egyptian, the Babylonian, and the Persian rose, filled the planet with sound and splendor, then faded to dream-stuff and passed away; the Greek and the Roman followed, and made a vast noise, and they are gone; other peoples have sprung up and held their torch high for a time, but it burned out, and they sit in twilight now, or have vanished.

The Jew saw them all, beat them all, and is now what he always was, exhibiting no decadence, no infirmities of age, no weakening of his parts, no slowing of his energies, no dulling of his alert and aggressive mind. All things are mortal but the Jew; all other forces pass, but he remains. What is the secret of his immortality?

About Jerusalem

For the Jews:
  Location of the Temple built by Solomon (2 Chronicles 3:1-2)
  Located in the land promised by God
  Capital of Israel

For Christians:
  Location of death and resurrection of Jesus Christ.
  (Matthew 27:32-28:15, Mark 15:21-16:19, Luke 23:26-24:53, John 19:16-20:30)

For Muslims:
  Location of Dome of the Rock, a Muslim shrine that was built on the Temple Mount (Mount Moriah) in Jerusalem in 691 CE.

NOTES:

1. Dimont, Max I., Jews, God, and History. (New American Library, 1962). 424

2. Dimont, 416

3. Karsh, Efraim. *1948, Israel and the Palestinians: The True Story*, Commentary Magazine, 2008 https://www.commentarymagazine.com/articles/1948-israel-and-the-palestinians-annotated-text/ Accessed 19 November 2016.

4. Israeli National Anthem – "Hatikvah" https://www.youtube.com/watch?v=1DPqNHkm1bM Accessed Feb 4, 2017

5. Wikipedia *"Egypt-Israel Peace Treaty"*. Accessed 18 November 2016.

6. Wikipedia *"Religion in Israel"*. Accessed 18 November 2016.

7. Mikhael, Mary. *Joshua: A Journey of Faith*, Horizons Bible Study 2009-2010. (Presbyterian Women, Presbyterian Church U.S.A.), 24

8. Dimont, 434

9. Vital Statistics: Latest Population Statistics for Israel. http://www.jewishvirtuallibrary.org/jsource/Society_&_Culture/newpop.html Accessed 19 November 2016.

10. Twain, Mark, *Concerning the Jews,* published Harper's Magazine, March 1898 (excerpts) http://aperfectworldnow.blogspot.com/2009/04/mark-twain-concerning-jews-1898.html Accessed Feb 4, 2017

Lesson 10: So what, why study Joshua? Lessons Learned

OBJECTIVE:

Analyze what you believe and make a commitment to pass this story on to the next generation.

Joshua is a great story of a major event in the life of the Hebrew people; a story about what happens when people are obedient to the LORD.

SUGGESTED HYMN:

I Love to Tell the Story

QUESTIONS:

1. What are some attributes of God as found in Joshua?

2. Is "trust and obey" still good advice today? Why?

3. Remembering - Why tell your children? Why "tell the story"?
Why didn't the next generation know the LORD and what He had done for Israel?
How can we make sure we don't repeat this?

4. What we believe matters (Do you understand the concept of Worldviews).

5. How has this study changed your thinking about who God is and how he works with his people?

ADDITIONAL INFORMATION:

Attributes of God

God is Sovereign
Keeps his promise
Holy
Faithful
Gracious
Provides guidance
Expects obedience

"Trust and Obey" is still good advice today

In Joshua, the lesson is listen to God, be obedient and experience God's favor, be sinful and experience God's wrath. Here are a few additional thoughts.

1. We live in a "broken" world. Just like the story of Achan, regardless of our ability to be obedient we are also affected by the actions of others.

> These things I have spoken to you, that in Me you may have peace. In the world you will have tribulation; but be of good cheer, I have overcome the world." (John 16:33)

2. Sin has consequences. For example: If you take drugs, give in to anger, are unable to forgive you will have trouble. Don't fight the Devil alone, help is available, trust God to help.

3. When things are not going well, God may be trying to get your attention. Sin is not necessarily what we are doing but what we are not doing.

Blaise Pascal said "diversion and indifference are the Devil's two most successful weapons against faith and salvation, the two widest roads to Hell in today's world" [1]

Why pass on the "stories" to the next generation?

The current world exposes us to many ideas, for each of us we need to spend time thinking about what we believe and why. For parents, this is particularly important; since parents have the responsibility to pass on the story and guidelines for living on to their children (please don't abdicate this responsibility to the public school system!).

What is a Worldview? [2]

A worldview is a theory of the world, used for living in the world. A worldview is a mental model of reality — a framework of ideas & attitudes about the world, ourselves, and life, a comprehensive system of beliefs — with answers for a wide range of questions:

What are humans, why we are here, and what is our purpose in life?

What are your goals for life?

When you make decisions about using time, what are your values and priorities?

What can we know, and how? And with how much certainty.

Does reality include only matter/energy, or is there more?

A worldview includes our assumptions about God:

Can we know whether God exists? Does God exist?
If so, what characteristics does God have, and what relationship with the universe?

Have miracles occurred in the past, as claimed in the Bible, and do they occur now?

Are natural events produced and guided by God?

Does God communicate with us (mentally and spiritually) in everyday life, and through written revelation, as in the Bible?

What is God's role in history?   Is there a purpose and meaning in history, for each of us individually and for all of us together, or is life just a long string of things happening?

What happens after death?

Worldview is more than culture, even though the distinction between the two can sometimes be subtle. It extends to perceptions of time and space, of happiness and well-being. The beliefs, values, and behaviors of a culture stem directly from its worldview.

More Information about Worldview[3]

How might growing up in the modern global village both facilitate and cripple my understanding of the gospel?

What aspects of my family background, language, political philosophy, media exposure, gender, ecclesiastical heritage, national history, psychological make-up and other cultural and personal characteristics aid and obstruct my understanding of Scripture and its central message?

What are the personal and cultural lenses through which I read the Bible?

What aspects of Scripture do they bring into clear focus? What aspects do they blur or skew?

Examples of Biblical Beliefs and Values

"I am the way and the truth and the life. No one comes to the Father except through Me." (John 14:6)

"For all have sinned and fall short of the glory of God." (Romans 3:23)

"the chief dangers of the 20th century Church would be politics without God, Heaven without Hell, forgiveness without repentance, salvation without regeneration, religion without the Holy Spirit, and Christianity without Christ" William Booth[4]

Examples of Non-Biblical Beliefs and Values

All paths lead to God.

People are born good, they are corrupted by society.

Ends justify the means.

He who dies with the most toys, wins.

Humans are the chance product of a biological process of evolution.

Truth is relative to one's culture.

NOTES:

1. Kreeft, Peter, *Christianity for Modern Pagans - Pascal's Pensées,* (Ignatius Press, 1993), 188

2. Rusbult, Craig. Wh*at is a Worldview? - Definition & Introduction,*
http://www.asa3.org/ASA/education/views/index.html
The American Scientific Affiliation
Accessed 19 November 2016

3. Hall, Christopher A., *Reading Scripture with the Church Fathers,* (IVP Academic, 1998).

4. Booth, William, Founder of the Salvation Army (1829-1916).

The Gospel (Good News)[1]

This study should help you learn about God's plans, about how humans respond and the results. The story of Joshua is a high point in the story of God's relationship with the people of Israel. Unfortunately the people did not follow God's directions as can be learned by reading Judges. Fortunately God has not given up on us. Here's the Good News.

God's Design

God created us in His own image to be His friend and to experience a full life assured of His love. God loves you.

> *So God created man in His own image; in the image of God He created him; male and female He created them.* (Genesis 1:27)

Humanity's Problem - Sin

Humans have chosen to disobey God and thus are separated from Him.

> *So God looked upon the earth, and indeed it was corrupt; for all flesh had corrupted their way on the earth.* (Genesis: 6:12)

> *For all have sinned and fall short of the glory of God.* (Romans 3:23)

> *For the wages of sin is death, but the gift of God is eternal life in Christ Jesus our LORD.* (Romans 6:23)

God's Remedy – Jesus Christ

On our own, we cannot bridge the gap. Christ's death alone bridges the gulf between God and human beings.

> *For Christ also suffered once for sins, the just for the unjust, that He might bring us to God,* (1 Peter 3:18)

> *But God demonstrates His own love toward us, in that while we were still sinners, Christ died for us.* (Romans 5:8)

Your Response - Repent and Believe

Acknowledge your sinfulness, trust Christ's forgiveness, and allow God to guide your life.

> *For God so loved the world that He gave His only begotten Son, that whoever believes in Him should not perish but have everlasting life.* (John 3:16)

> *If you love me, keep My commandments. And I will pray the Father, and He will give you another Helper, that He may abide with you forever - the Spirit of truth,* (John 14:15-16)

> *But the fruit of the Spirit is love, joy, peace, longsuffering, kindness, goodness, faithfulness, gentleness, self-control.* (Galatians 5:22-23)

So... what is your response?

> *I call heaven and earth as witnesses today against you, that I have set before you life and death, blessing and cursing; therefore choose life, that both you and your descendants may live;* (Deuteronomy 30:19)

Some suggestions for learning more:

Read at least one of these books in the Bible:
> Matthew, Mark, Luke or John.
> If the book you read does not make sense, read it again.

Ask God for guidance and direction. You can talk to God anytime, he is always listening.

Say this prayer –

"Thank you, God, for loving me, and for sending your Son to die for my sins. I repent of my sins and receive Jesus Christ as my personal Savior. And now as your child, I turn my entire life over to you. Amen.[2]

NOTES:

1. Based on the Navigators "Bridge to Life"
   http://navresources.ca/page.php?page=bridge
   Accessed 19 November 2016

2. Karon, Jan. *At Home in Mitford*, 1996, (Penguin Books, 1994), 184

Truehearted, Wholehearted (Lesson 2)

Truehearted, wholehearted, faithful and loyal,
King of our lives, by Thy grace we will be;
Under the standard exalted and royal,
Strong in thy strength we will battle for Thee.

Truehearted, wholehearted, fullest allegiance
Yielding henceforth to our glorious King;
Valiant endeavor and loving obedience,
Freely and joyously now would we bring.

Truehearted, wholehearted, Savior all glorious!
Take Thy great power and reign there alone,
Over our wills and affections victorious,
Freely surrendered and wholly Thine own.

Refrain:
Peal out the watchword! Silence it never!
Song of our spirits, rejoicing and free;
Peal out the watchword! Loyal forever!
King of our lives, by thy grace we will be.

Amen.

Words for Truehearted, Wholehearted
by Frances R. Havergal 1836 - 1879

Frances' father was a clergyman (Anglican). Frances was born in England. She was educated in both England and Germany. She was proficient in Hebrew, Greek, French, German and Italian. Frances was a natural musician. She was a concert soloist, played the piano and wrote many hymns.

Trust and Obey (Lesson 4)

When we walk with the Lord, in the light of his Word,
What a glory he sheds on our way!
While we do his good will, he abides with us still,
And with all who will trust and obey.

Not a burden we bear, not a sorrow we share,
But our toil he doth richly repay;
Not a grief or a loss, not a frown or a cross,
But is blest if we trust and obey.

But we never can prove the delights of his love
Until all on the altar we lay;
For the favor he shows and the joy he bestows
Are for them who will trust and obey.

Then in fellowship sweet we will sit at his feet,
Or will walk by his side in the way;
What he says we will do, where he sends we will go;
Never fear, only trust and obey.

Refrain:
Trust and obey, for there's no other way
To be happy in Jesus, but to trust and obey.

Amen.

Words for Trust and Obey by Rev. John H. Sammis 1846 - 1919

Rev. Sammis was born in Brooklyn, NY and was a successful business man in Indiana.
In 1880 he was ordained as a Presbyterian minister and later taught at Bible Institute of
Los Angeles (BIOLA).

God of our Fathers (Lesson 6)

God of our fathers, whose almighty hand
Leads forth in beauty all the starry band
Of shining worlds in splendor through the skies
Our grateful songs before Thy throne arise.

Thy love divine hath led us in the past,
In this free land by Thee our lot is cast,
Be Thou our Ruler, Guardian, Guide and Stay,
Thy Word our law, Thy paths our chosen way.

From war's alarms, from deadly pestilence,
Be Thy strong arm our ever sure defense;
Thy true religion in our hearts increase,
Thy bounteous goodness nourish us in peace.

Refresh Thy people on their toilsome way,
Lead us from night to never ending day;
Fill all our lives with love and grace divine,
And glory, laud, and praise be ever Thine.

Words by Daniel C. Roberts, 1876
George W. Warren, organist of St. Thomas' Church, New York
He wrote the tune for the centennial celebration of the United States Constitution.

Daniel Roberts was born on Long Island, New York, in 1841. Daniel attended college in Ohio and served as a private with the eighty-fourth Ohio Volunteers during the War Between the States. As the war ended, he was ordained as a deacon in the Presbyterian Episcopalian church and shortly afterward as a priest. He served for the next thirty years pastoring Episcopalian churches in New England, including a decades-long pastorate of St. Paul's Church in Concord, New Hampshire.

George Warren, originally pursued a business career. But his natural talent soon shoved him into music, and he eventually became one of American's premier organists. During his career, he served various congregations in New York City. George died in 1902.

I Love to Tell the Story (Lesson 10)

I love to tell the story of unseen things above,
Of Jesus and his glory, of Jesus and his love.
I love to tell the story, because I know 'tis true;
It satisfies my longings as nothing else can do.

I love to tell the story; more wonderful it seems
Than all the golden fancies of all our golden dreams.
I love to tell the story, it did so much for me;
And that is just the reason I tell it now to thee.

I love to tell the story; 'Tis pleasant to repeat
What seems, each time I tell it, more wonderfully sweet.
I love to tell the story, for some have never heard
The message of salvation, from God's own holy Word.

I love to tell the story, for those who know it best
Seem hungering and thirsting, to hear it like the rest.
I love to tell the story, I sing the new, new song,
'Twill be the old, old story that I have loved so long.

Refrain:
I love to tell the story, 'Twill be my theme in glory,
To tell the old, old story, of Jesus and his love.

Amen.

Words to I Love to Tell the Story by A. Katherine Hankey 1834 – 1911.

Katherine was born into the home of a wealthy English banker and a member of the Anglican Church. She was inspired by the Methodist revival of John Wesley and organized and taught in Sunday schools in London. She then did missionary work as a nurse in Africa, assisting her brother. When Kate was only 30 years old, she experienced a serious illness. It was during that time she wrote a poem, The Story Told" which became the basic part of "I Love to Tell the Story". She recovered from the illness and lived to the age of 77.

Bibliography/Resources

Commentaries

Boling, Robert G. and Ernest G. Wright, *JOSHUA a new translation with introduction and commentary - The Anchor Bible, Volume 6.* Doubleday, 1982.

Enns, Paul P., *Joshua: Bible Study Commentary.* Zondervan, 1981.

Navigators, *A Life-changing encounter with God's Word from the book of Joshua.* NavPress, 2013.

Wiersbe, Warren W., *Be Strong (an Old Testament Study, Joshua).* David C. Cook, 1993.

Books, Articles & DVDs

Bible Atlas or Maps in a Study Bible

Collins, Larry and Lapierre, Dominique. *O Jerusalem.* Simon and Schuster, 1972.

Dimont, Max I., *Jews, God and History.* New American Library, 1962.

Gumbel, Nicky, *the Jesus Lifestyle.* Alpha,1993.

Hahn, Jerome S., *Bible Basics: Introduction & Reference Guide to the Five Books of Moses.* International Traditions Corp., 2008.

Mahoney, Timothy P., *Patterns of Evidence: Exodus.* Thinking Man Films, 2015 (DVD).

Michener, James A., T*he Source.* Random House, 1965.

Mikhael, Mary, *Joshua: a Journey of Faith,* Horizons Bible Study 2009-2010. Presbyterian Women, Presbyterian Church (U.S.A.).

Murray, Andrew, *Abiding in Christ.* BethanyHouse, 1895.

Rohl, David, *From Eden to Exile: The Epic History of the People of the Bible,* Arrow Books, 2002.

Sproul, R.C., *Pleasing God,* Tyndale, 1988.

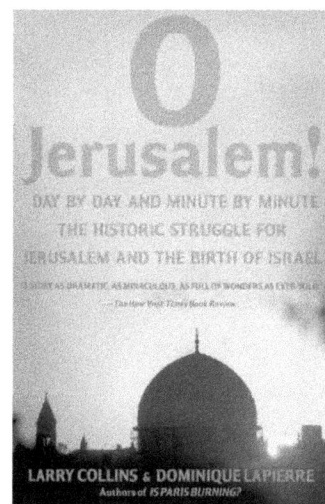

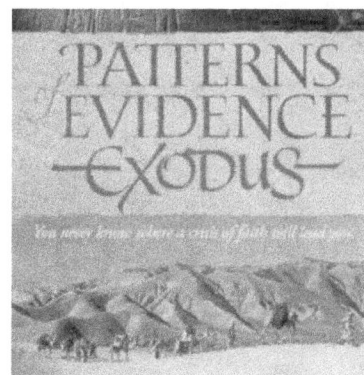

Illustrations

Historical and Literary Context
> Joshua's Covenant Stone at Shechem
> (Source: Google images)

> Map Ancient Near East
> > (Source: Bible History OnLine   www.bible-history.com)

What do we know about Josua?
> Joshua, artist unknown (photo found on internet)
> > (Source: www.RhythmOnTheRock.com)

> Jordan River in springtime
> > (Source: Google images)

The Battle of Jericho
> Battle of Jericho, James Tissot
> > (Source: WikiArt.org - public domain)

The Law
> Ten Commandments - Tablets
> > (Source: Google images)

The Land Is Divided, Unfinished Business
> Map of the Land - prior to Conquest
> > (Source: Bible History OnLine
> > www.bible-history.com)

> Map of the Land - shows the allocation of land to the tribes
> > (Source: Bible History OnLine
> > www.bible-history.com)

> Picture of the Land
> > (Source: taken 2009, by C. V. Kirkstadt, view of Galilee)

The Land
> The Levant
> > (Source: Google images)

So What? Why Study Joshua?
> Picture of "Sowing Seeds"
> > Source: Picture of Bronze Sculpture located at
> > > Mountain View Presbyterian Church in Loveland, Colorado.
> > Artist: Sutton Betti.
> > The inspiration for this sculpture was the
> > > Parable of the Sower (Matthew 13:1-23, Luke 8:4-15)

About the Author

I am a senior citizen living in Loveland, Colorado. I was raised in a Christian home and for many years took for granted the many blessings that living as a Christian afforded. In the last 20 years, I have attended various Bible Studies and provided support for Church Libraries at two churches.

In 2009, I facilitated a Bible Study on Joshua, using the Horizons Study published by Presbyterian Women, Presbyterian Church (U.S.A.). The notes from this project are the basis for this Bible Study Guide.

C. V. Kirkstadt
2017